Introduction to
the Lotus Sutra

by
Shinjo Suguro

Translated by
Nichiren Buddhist International Center

Revised by
Daniel B. Montgomery

JAIN PUBLISHING COMPANY
Fremont, California

Jain Publishing Company is a diversified publisher of books and related products covering subject areas such as business/management, foods/cooking, health/healing, motivation/inspiration, self-help/psychology and religions/philosophies. Additionally, under our imprint, **Asian Humanities Press**, we publish scholarly as well as general interest books in the subjects of Asian religions/philosophies and languages/literature. A complete, up to date listing of all our products, with color illustrations, descriptions, review excerpts, specifications and prices is always available on-line at our web site at the following address:

http://www.jainpub.com

We invite you to browse through our on-line catalog from time to time to find out what is available and what is forthcoming. We also encourage you to communicate your comments and suggestions to us via e-mail. Our e-mail address is mail@jainpub.com.

Library of Congress Cataloging-in-Publication Data

Suguro, Shinjō. 1925–
    An introduction to the Lotus Sutra / revised by Daniel B. Montgomery.
        p.   cm.
    ISBN 0-87573-078-7 (pbk. : alk. paper)
    1. Tripiṭaka. Sūtrapiṭaka. Saddharmapuṇḍarīkasūtra—Introductions.   I. Montgomery, Daniel B.
BQ2057.S877   1998
294.3'85—dc21   98–15226
                                                                       CIP

CONTENTS

NOTES ON THE REVISION

In general, our revision of the text has sought to make the translation more understandable to an English-speaking reader, especially for one who may not be familiar with Buddhist terminology.

Sanskrit terms have been avoided whenever possible, or introduced only when accompanied by English translations. The word *dharma*, for instance, is familiar to scholars but easily misunderstood by a general reader. William Soothill's *Dictionary of Chinese Buddhist Terms* gives no fewer than seven meanings for *dharma*. It has other meanings in Hinduism. To the average English-speaking reader, it probably means a kind of Oriental teaching (which, indeed, is Soothill's seventh definition). Many centuries ago, Chinese translators decided to avoid this ambiguous word and translate it according to context, generally by the word "law." We have followed their good example. The reader may be familiar with such terms as natural law, cosmic law, and moral law, all of which are close to the most common uses of the Buddhist term *dharma*. We have resorted to *dharma* only near the end of the book, when the reader may find himself ready to accept some of its ambiguities.

We have also avoided the term *Tathagata*, a title of the Buddha, the meaning of which is unclear even in Sanskrit. It is almost certain to be mispronounced. According to Professor Leon Hurvitz, "Without much doubt, *Tathagata* is a non-Indic word refurbished to have an Indic appearance long after it had come into current use among India's Buddhists." We have avoided the term whenever possible, by simply saying "Buddha" instead.

Translating long Sanskrit names into Chinese and thence to English can result in more than one rendering of the same names. We have generally followed the version of Bishop Murano, whose text was used by the translators. Sometimes, however, we have turned to other translators for help, or used our own judgment. On a few occasions, we have gone back to the original Sanskrit.

Chinese and Japanese Buddhist technical terms have been rendered according to Bishop Murano's *Manual of Nichiren Buddhism* (Tokyo: Nichiren Shu Headquarters, 1995), the *Japanese-English Buddhist Dictionary* (Tokyo: Daito Shuppansha, 1965), or *The Essentials of Buddhist Philosophy* by Junjiro Takakusu (Third Edition, Honolulu: University of Hawaii, 1956). For the term *Hommon*, however, which literally means "Primal Gate," I prefer "Primal Mystery." *Gohonzon* has no exact English equivalent, and translators have rendered it in different ways. Here I follow Bishop Murano's, "Most-Venerable-One."

From time to time I have inserted comments in brackets. Although these insertions were not in the Japanese original, I hope they will clarify some points which may not be clear to the English-speaking reader.

I have made a few corrections of minor nature in Rev. Suguro's text; corrections which I am sure he would have made himself had they been brought to his attention. Except for the bracketed insertions, however, the text is substantially his.

Daniel B. Montgomery
Kerrville, Texas, 1995

NOTE TO THE READER

1. The original text of this book is *Hokekyo Kogi*, vols. 1 & 2, written by Shinjo Suguro in Japanese language, published in 1993 by Nichiren-Shu Shinbunsha.

2. The English translation of the *Lotus Sutra* referred to is Senchu Murano's *The Sutra of the Lotus Flower of the Wonderful Dharma*, second edition, published in 1991 by Nichiren-Shu, Tokyo.

3. All the Sanskrit words transliterated into Chinese characters are given in Sanskrit.

4. All the Chinese words transliterated into Chinese characters are given in the Chinese pronunciation.

5. All the Japanese words transliterated into Chinese characters are given in the Japanese pronunciation.

6. The Japanese pronunciation is also used for the dharanis given in Chapters XXVI and XXVIII.

An Overview

The most complete collection of Buddhist scriptures, the Taisho Edition, consists of 3,497 works. Among them, 1,487 are called *sutras*, and consist of sermons preached by the Buddha. Among these more than a thousand sutras, the Lotus Sutra, or *Sutra of the Lotus Flower of the Wonderful Law*, is the most popular and best known. When Buddhism was introduced into Japan in the mid-sixth century, Prince Shotoku lectured on this sutra and wrote a book on it called *Hokke Gisho* (*A Commentary on the Lotus Sutra*). About two hundred years later, in the early Heian Period (794-1185), Saicho, who is also known as Great Master Dengyo, established a Buddhist school on Mt. Hiei, whence he propagated the Lotus teachings throughout the country. His school, the Tendai ("Heavenly Terrace"), was for many centuries the most influential in the country. Eisai, founder of the Rinzai Zen Sect, Dogen, founder of the Soto Zen Sect, Honen, founder of the Pure Land Sect (*Jodo Shu*), and Shinran, founder of the True Pure Land Sect (*Jodo Shin Shu*), the founders of new movements during the Kamakura Period (1185-1333), all studied the Lotus Sutra at Mt. Hiei. Their own sectarian doctrines, however, were not based upon it directly.

Nichiren, who also studied the Lotus Sutra there, founded his sect on doctrines resting squarely on faith in the Lotus Sutra. He devoted his whole life to advocating it and putting its teachings into practice. While other Buddhist sects today read it as a supplemental scripture, the Nichiren lineage considers the Lotus Sutra to be its basic text.

The Lotus Sutra has had much influence in Japan, not only on religion, but also on art and literature. Many Japanese classics, such as *Makura-no-Soshi* by Seisho Nagon, *The Tale of Genji* by Murasaki Shikibu, *The Tale of Heike*, and the *Konjaku Story*, often refer to it. Since ancient times, authors composed many *tanka* (31-syllable Japanese poems), called *Shakkyoka*, whose themes were derived from lectures on the sutra. Devout laymen and women also copied sutras by hand as pious exercises. Many times they borrowed themes from the Lotus Sutra. Some hand-written copies of the Lotus Sutra, beautifully illustrated and ornamented, have great importance in the history of Japanese art. Particularly well known is the one called *Heike-Nokyo*, which is dedicated to the Itsukushima Shrine.

The sutras were originally written in Sanskrit, the sacred Language of India, and later translated into Chinese. The Sutra of the Lotus Flower of the Wonderful Law (*Saddharma-pundarika-sutra*) was translated by Kumarajiva, a distinguished scholar from Kucha in Central Asia. In 401 he was invited to the capital city of Ch'ang-an by Emperor Yao Hsing. From then until his death about ten years later, he supervised the translation of numerous sutras into Chinese. He did the *Saddharma-pundarika-sutra* in 406, rendering it into an elegant Chinese version which quickly became popular. He named it, *Miao-fa-lien-hua-ching*, which in Japanese is pronounced *Myoho Renge Kyo.**

Kumarajiva was not the only one to translate the sutra. In 286 Dharmaraksha had made a translation which he called *Sho-Hokkekyo, The True Lotus Sutra*. Unfortunately, it was difficult to understand and not widely read. In 601 Dharmagupta and Jnanagupta made another version called *Tempon Myoho Renge Kyo*; in it they made some changes in Kumarajiva's text and added a chapter which was discovered later. (This chapter is now included in the Kumarajiva text.) Three more versions are said to have been made but were lost in time. Today only Kumarajiva's rendering is still popular.

---

* Because Chinese is written with ideograms instead of letters, Japanese scholars, accustomed to these same ideograms used in writing their own language, were able to read the Chinese texts by giving them a Japanese pronunciation.

A copy of the sutra in Sanskrit was preserved and transmitted in Nepal. A revised Sanskrit version has recently been published there, and some modern Japanese translations from the Sanskrit have also been published. There are several translations available in English, both from Sanskrit and Chinese.

As we said, the Lotus Sutra was originally called *Saddharma-pundarika-sutra* in Sanskrit. *Saddharma* means the "wonderful Dharma," and *pundarika* is rendered "lotus flower" by Kumarajiva. *Sad* means "righteousness" or "truth." *Dharma*, the essential idea of Buddhism in various contexts, means in this case, "the law," "the truth," or "the teaching of the truth." Therefore, literally *Saddharma* means "righteous teaching" or "righteous truth."

You may wonder why we dare call this particular teaching "righteous" or "true" when we know that every single teaching of the Buddha is true. What does "righteous truth" imply? Because the Lotus Sutra reveals to us the principal and deepest teachings of the Buddha, people have tried to name it by expressing its special importance. Instead of saying, "the true truth," Kumarajiva used the word *myo*, a word with an esoteric quality in Chinese meaning "noble richness" or "marvelous." Therefore, he translated *Saddharma* as the "wonderful" or "marvelous" Dharma. *Pundarika* means 'the lotus flower," particularly the white lotus flower. We compare something wonderful and excellent with the lotus flower. So *Saddharma pundarika* represents "the righteous (wonderful) Dharma as marvelous as lotus flowers." At the same time, the lotus flower symbolizes the most important Bodhisattva practices in Mahayana Buddhism. In Chapter Fifteen, "Bodhisattvas from Underground," it says:

> The Buddha's children have studied the way of Bodhisattvas well. They are no more defiled by worldliness just as a lotus flower is not defiled by water.

The lovely lotus flower grows out of muddy water and is not defiled by it. In the same way, Bodhisattvas, persons who put the Buddha's teachings into practice, can live in the midst of a world defiled by vice and corruption, and yet not be contaminated by it. They can teach and awaken other people while keeping their own minds pure. They can save others, however, only when they live with them here in this evil world.

The Lotus Sutra consists of twenty-eight chapters. At the beginning, the Buddha taught from Mount Sacred Eagle (*Grdhrakuta*, "Vulture Peak," in Sanskrit) near the city of Rajagriha, India, which today is called Rajgir. In Chapter Eleven, "Beholding the Stupa of Treasures," he ascended to the sky and remained there until returning to Mt. Sacred Eagle in Chapter Twenty-three, "The Previous Life of Medicine-King Bodhisattva." Thus he held three assemblies, which are called the First Assembly on Mt. Sacred Eagle; the Assembly in the Sky; and the Second Assembly on Mt. Sacred Eagle. We can divide the chapters of the sutra into three parts according to these three locations.

Since ancient times, however, the Lotus Sutra has been accompanied by two other sutras. The first, *The Sutra of In-numerable Teachings* is called, "The Opening Sutra," and is placed at the beginning. The other, *The Sutra of Beholding the Practices of the Bodhisattva Samantabhadra*, is called, "The Closing Sutra," and is placed at the end. When the three are joined together, they become the "Threefold Lotus Sutra" or "Lotus Trilogy." We, like others before us, will treat them as one unit.

The Opening Sutra of the Threefold Lotus Sutra

THE SUTRA OF INNUMERABLE TEACHINGS

Before explaining the twenty-eight chapters of the *Sutra of the Lotus Flower of the Wonderful Law*, we must say more about "The Threefold Lotus Sutra." When the Lotus Sutra is accompanied by the opening and closing sutras, the Lotus Trilogy consists of the following:

The Opening Sutra:
   One volume of *The Sutra of Innumerable Teachings*, in three chapters, translated by Dharma-jatayasas during the Ch'i Dynasty in 481.

The Main Sutra:
   Eight volumes of *The Sutra of the Lotus Flower of the Wonderful Law*, in 28 chapters, translated by Kumarajiva during the Later Ch'in Dynasty in 406, and including the additional chapter added later.

The Closing Sutra:
   One volume of *The Sutra of Beholding the Practices of the Bodhisattva Samantabhadra*, in one chapter, translated by Dharmamitra during the Yüan-chia era (424-453) of the Liu Sung Dynasty.

The Opening Sutra heralds and the Closing Sutra concludes the Main Sutra. Chih-i, the great scholar and founder of the Chinese Tendai Sect, based all his teachings on the Threefold Lotus Sutra. Nichiren often referred to "the ten volumes of the Lotus Sutra." Obviously, by "ten volumes," he means

the eight composing the Lotus Sutra itself and one each from
the opening and closing sutras. From ancient times, people
have been accustomed to reciting them together.

Let us begin with *The Sutra of Innumerable Teachings.*
We will take up the Closing Sutra afterwards.

According to Chapter I of the Lotus Sutra, "Introduction,"
the Buddha expounded a sutra called "Innumerable Teachings" before presenting the Lotus Sutra, and then entered into
its *samadhi* (deep concentration on its theme). During this
time his body and mind were motionless. The "innumerable
teachings" mentioned here are the same as *The Sutra of Innumerable Teachings,* the Opening Sutra. It consists of three
chapters: "Virtues," (Chapter I), "Preaching," (Chapter II), and
"Ten Merits," (Chapter III).

Chapter I: VIRTUES

The contents of the first chapter, "Virtues," are devoted
to praising the good qualities of Bodhisattvas and especially
the virtues of the Buddha. A Bodhisattva is a practitioner who
seeks enlightenment not only for himself but for others. Their
teacher, the historical Buddha, who lived in India from 565 to
486 B.C., is generally known in the East by his title, Sakyamuni, the "Sage of the Sakya clan."

Sakyamuni expounded this sutra, as he did the Lotus
Sutra, on Mt. Sacred Eagle near Rajagriha, India. He was
accompanied by twelve thousand great *bhikshus* (monks),
who were called *sravakas* (hearers), eighty thousand Bodhisattvas, and others. The main person addressed during his
sermon was a Bodhisattva named Great-Adornment. (The
numbers, of course, are symbolic.) The Buddha is said to
have preached 80,000 sermons—one for each Bodhisattva,
no two of whom were alike. And the monks practiced a
twelve-fold discipline, called *dhuta.*

The eighty thousand Bodhisattvas who were present
had already attained deep wisdom and the knowledge of
emancipation; in their actions, they were like Buddhas. Be-

cause they sought to save all living beings from sufferings, they had well-deserved titles like Great-Leader, Great-Mariner, and Great-Physician. Great-Adornment Bodhisattva, noting how all the people in the assembly enjoyed mental tranquillity, arose from his seat and led the others up to the Buddha. He bowed before the Buddha's feet, burned incense, and scattered celestial flowers, robes, and jewels before him. Joining their hands together reverently, he and the other Bodhisattvas praised the Buddha in verse. His words are the highlight of this chapter. He begins by saying:

> (The Buddha's) moral breeze and virtuous fragrance deeply permeate all.
> Serene is his wisdom, calm his emotion, and stable his prudence.
> His thought is settled, his (discriminating) consciousness is extinct,
> And so his mind is quiet.

These are but three of the many lines in which he proclaims his admiration for Sakyamuni Buddha. Just as the scent of flowers permeates everything around it, he says, so the Buddha's moral influence pervades all living beings who approach him. The very presence of the Buddha is his most effective teaching. There are many ways of teaching, such as laying down rules for people to follow, setting them free, reproaching them, praising them, or being didactic. But the best way of all is by one's own dynamic presence—teaching by example instead of by words. This, he says, is how the Buddha teaches.

The Bodhisattva also says that the Buddha has entered into a special state of mind, called *dhyana*-concentration. In this state, one's mind is calm and feels no emotional irritation. "Serene is his wisdom," says Great-Adornment Bodhisattva, "calm his emotion, and stable his prudence."

By practicing *dhyana*-concentration, even we ordinary people can achieve a spirit of not being attached to emotional

passions or irritants, and we can see things clearly just as they
are. Because the Buddha achieved the highest level of this
concentration, he eliminated every relative concept which
could cause attachment to worldly things and prejudice his
judgment. Thus to him, all relationships, such as existence
and non-existence, birth and death, long and short, this and
that, are relative, not absolute. He sees this because "his
thought is settled, his (discriminating) consciousness is extinct, and his mind is quiet."

After singing the praises of the Buddha, the chapter ends
by saying that because, in his previous existences, the World-
Honored One diligently practiced all manner of virtues to
bring benefits to us living beings, he has become the Buddha,
the Fully Enlightened One.

Chapter II: PREACHING

The second chapter, "Preaching," tells us what kind of
sutras the Buddha has expounded.

Speaking on behalf of the eighty thousand Bodhisattvas,
Great-Adornment says to Sakyamuni that he has a special
question to ask him. The Buddha replies, "I am happy to hear
that. Soon I will leave this world and enter into *parinirvana*
(perfect quietude). I do not want you to have any doubts
then. Ask me now whatever it is you want to know. I will
answer all your questions."

Then Bodhisattva Great-Adornment and the other
Bodhisattvas ask him:

World-Honored One! If the Bodhisattvas want to attain perfect enlightenment quickly, what teaching should they practice?

Sakyamuni answers:

Good sons! There is a Dharma (teaching/truth) called the
Innumerable Teachings. If a Bodhisattva learns it and masters

it, he will be able to attain perfect enlightenment. While he is learning it, he should observe that all existences are empty (*sunya*) by nature; they are neither big nor small, neither appearing nor disappearing, neither fixed nor mobile, neither advancing nor retreating; they are non-dual, just like the emptiness of the sky. Living beings, however, habitually discriminate falsely, saying, "It is this," or "It is that," and "It is advantageous," or "It is disadvantageous." They entertain evil thoughts, make various evil *karma* (actions causing reactions), migrate within the six realms of existence, and suffer from miseries from which they cannot escape. Observing this, the Bodhisattva should feel compassion for them, display great mercy to relieve them from suffering, and penetrate deeply into the law in order to save them. As the natural desires of living beings are innumerable, so the Buddha's preaching is immeasurable, and as the preaching is immeasurable, so the teachings are innumerable. Such innumerable teachings, however, originate from the one law (Truth), which has no form.

Good sons! If you correctly practice Innumerable Teachings of the Dharma, you will attain perfect enlightenment without fail. I am telling you, if the Bodhisattvas want to attain perfect enlightenment quickly, they should practice the Sutra of Innumerable Teachings.

Great-Adornment Bodhisattva then said to Sakyamuni:

World-Honored One! Your teaching is very deep and profound. The natures of living beings and the teaching of emancipation are also wonderful. Since you attained enlightenment, those who heard your teaching have reached different stages of enlightenment. But if there is no difference between the truth in your past teaching and that in the present, why do you say that only those who practice the Sutra of Innumerable Teachings can attain enlightenment so quickly? World-Honored One! Please clarify this, so we will not be so perplexed.

Sakyamuni replied:

> You have asked me a very good question. After I practiced austerities for six years, I sat under the bodhi tree and attained enlightenment. Now that I see with the eyes of a Buddha, I realize that the natures and desires of all living beings are not the same. For that reason, I have expounded the law in various ways according to the capacities of different living beings. I do this by the skillful expedients. During the forty or so years since then, I have not yet revealed the ultimate truth. That is still to come. That is why no one has been able to attain Buddhahood quickly, even though they might have attained some degree of enlightenment by practicing various methods.

Sakyamuni said that, during the forty or so years since he became Buddha, he had expounded the Dharma in various ways but had not yet revealed the most precious truth. We know that he taught and led people for fifty years before entering nirvana (passing away) at the age of eighty. Therefore, the expression, "forty or so years," indicates that he was near the end of his life when he preached this sutra. During all of that time he had taught people by "skillful expedients" according to their capacities to understand. Now as he approached his final years, he was ready at last to reveal the universal truth.

The fact that someone who practices the Sutra of Innumerable Teachings can become a Buddha immediately simply proves that this sutra is the true teaching. Generally we need to practice for infinite ages in order to become a Buddha—a perfect and fully awakened human being. This, as we will explain later, is called the "practice for many eons." This sutra, however, says that by virtue of the Innumerable Teachings, we can become a Buddha right now. Although what becoming a Buddha immediately means is not explained precisely in this sutra, it is already obvious that the better the teachings are, the less time it takes to fulfill them. Only right teachings can obtain quick results. To become a Buddha immediately, or even in this very life, is one of the essential aims of Mahayana Buddhism. Sakyamuni continues:

> Good sons! Although the nature of water is one, a stream, a river, a well, a pond, a brook, and a great ocean are different from each other. Water takes many forms. The nature of the law is the same. It is one, but it can take on many different forms.
>
> Good sons! I preached the Four Noble Truths (the Wheel of the Dharma) for my first five disciples, Ajnata-Kaundinya and the others, at the Deer Park in Varanasi (modern Benares) after I rose from the terrace of enlightenment beneath the bodhi tree. Later I preached the Twelve Causes for those who would enlighten themselves (*Pratyekabuddhas*) and the Six Perfections (*paramitas*) for Bodhisattvas. Now I am preaching the Innumerable Teachings. On every occasion, because I have consistently taught that all things are void of any substance, the intent of the teaching has been the same. However, although the intent is the same, the teachings are different. These different teachings have led people to different levels of understanding. That is why my teaching up until now differs in the fruits of people's enlightenment.
>
> Good sons! I preached the Four Noble Truths for my monastic disciples (*sravakas*), the Twelve Causes for *Pratyekabuddhas*, and the Six Perfections for *Bodhisattvas*. Then for the Bodhisattvas I explained the practice extending over many eons. I taught them the twelve types of sutras of Great Extent, the Great Wisdom sutras (*Maha-Prajna*), and the Void of the Garland Sea (*Avatamsaka*). People who could understand those teachings reached different stages of enlightenment according to their particular capacities. The preaching is the same—enlightenment—but the meaning varies. As the meaning varies, so does the understanding of living beings. As the understanding varies, so do the fruits of enlightenment.

In Buddhism, there are three kinds of teachings known as The Three Vehicles. In the Lotus Trilogy, they are called the *Sravaka* Vehicle, the *Pratyekabuddha* Vehicle, and the Bodhisattva Vehicle. (A vehicle, of course, carries one to the "further shore.") The first two vehicles belong to "Lesser Vehicle" Buddhism (*Hinayana*), because they carry only the most highly gifted and motivated passengers. The Bodhisattva Vehicle, on the other hand, belongs to "Great Vehicle" Buddhism (*Mahayana*), so named because it can carry everyone without exception.

Several sutras are introduced here which are representative of the Great Vehicle. The "Sutras of Great Extent" mean the same thing. There are said to be twelve types of scripture: (1) *sutra*, prose discourses of the Buddha, (2) *geya*, verses repeating the substance of the prose discourses, (3) *gatha*, verses containing ideas not found in prose, (4) *nidana*, historical narratives, (5) *itivrttaka*, past lives of disciples of the Buddha, (6) *jataka*, past lives of the Buddha, (7) *adbhutadharma*, miracles performed by the Buddha, (8) *avadana*, allegories, (9) *upadesha*, doctrinal discussions, generally in question and answer form, (10) *udana*, statements made by the Buddha which are not prompted by questions from his disciples, (11) *vaipulya*, sutras dealing with broad topics, and (12) *vyakarana*, prophecies of the Buddha concerning the future Buddhahood of his disciples.

The *Maha-prajna-sutra* (The Sutra of Great Wisdom) is more properly titled, *Maha-prajna-paramita-sutra* (The Perfection of Great Wisdom). "Maha" means "great." "The Void of the Garland Sea" is the Garland Sutra, which contains teachings of the Buddha when he entered into the dhyana-concentration called the samadhi of the Seal of the Ocean or Ocean-imprint meditation. Every teaching of this sutra is devoted to explaining emptiness.

These sutras teach the Bodhisattva practices of the Great Vehicle. However, to reach the goal and become Buddhas requires long and diligent practice. *Kalpa* is a unit measuring an enormous length of time. There are several ways of explaining the length of a *kalpa*. According to one of them, suppose there is a castle ten cubic miles in size and filled with poppy seeds; now suppose someone removes one seed every hundred years; the length of a *kalpa* is the time it would take at this rate to remove all the seeds. A *kalpa*-long practice is how long it takes someone to become a Buddha.

The Sutra of Innumerable Teachings, however, says that *kalpa*-long practice is no longer necessary. By practicing this sutra, the Buddha says, one can become a Buddha immediately.

Chapter III: TEN MERITS

The third and final chapter of this short Sutra lists ten marvelous merits which enable people to attain perfect enlightenment quickly.

Great-Adornment Bodhisattva asks Sakyamuni:

This Sutra of Innumerable Teachings is truly wonderful and profound, and the law contained in it is reasonable in its logic and unsurpassed in its value. Once living beings can hear it, they will certainly acquire the great benefit to quickly attain Buddhahood. We all can see that this is the great direct way to enlightenment. World-Honored One! Out of your compassion for living beings, please explain why this sutra is so profound and inconceivable. Please explain where this sutra comes from, where it goes, and where it remains.

The "great direct way" is the way of practice to attain perfect enlightenment directly and immediately. Sakyamuni addresses Great-Adornment Bodhisattva:

This sutra is profound and inconceivable because it enables you to be able to uphold all the Law. In answer to your question of where this sutra comes from, where it goes, and where it remains: it originally comes from the abode of all the Buddhas, it goes to the aspiration of all living beings to Buddhahood, and it remains at the place where all Bodhisattvas practice.

Then the Buddha introduces the fact that this sutra contains ten marvelous merits. He presented them in numerical order, but since ancient times they have been called by the following names: (1) The Marvelous Power of a Pure Heart, (2) The Marvelous Power of Productive Teaching, (3) The Marvelous Power of a Mariner, (4) The Marvelous Power of a Prince, (5) The Marvelous Power of the Dragon's Children, (6) The Marvelous Power of Governing Fairly, (7) The Marvelous Power of Reward, (8) The Marvelous Power of Endurance, (9) The Marvelous Power of Salvation, and (10) The Marvelous Power of Ascending.

1. The Marvelous Power of a Pure Heart.

This sutra has merit that causes those who have not yet had faith to obtain it, and those who have not yet had compassion to acquire it. Furthermore it enables people to obtain the "four infinite virtues:" (1) infinite benevolence, giving happiness to others, (2) infinite compassion, removing the pain of others, (3) infinite sympathetic joy at the good fortune of others, (4) absolute impartiality, even towards one's enemies. It also gives them the heart to practice the Six Perfections.

2. The Marvelous Power of Productive Teaching.

If someone upholds even a verse or a phrase of this sutra, he or she will become conversant with hundreds of thousands of millions of innumerable teachings of the law. Just like a seed which produces hundreds of thousands of features, so the one law produces hundreds of thousands of millions of innumerable meanings. This is why it is called the Sutra of the Innumerable Teachings.

3. The Marvelous Power of a Mariner.

If people hear this sutra and uphold even one verse or phrase, they will become conversant with innumerable teachings and be able to practice them bravely, even if they navigate the "ten realms of existence" (different forms of human,

sub-human, and super-human life), which are defiled by desires. It is just like a mariner who is enabled to reach distant
shores if he is given passage on a better ship when he gets
too ill to sail his own. Likewise, if people follow the practice
of this Sutra of Innumerable teachings, by its power they will
be able to emancipate themselves from this world, which is
filled with confusion.

4. The Marvelous Power of a Prince.

Suppose there were a young prince, the lawful heir of
his parents, the King and Queen, but only seven years old.
Although he is still too young to govern his country, he is
respected by everyone as the Crown Prince. Likewise, those
who practice this sutra are like children born to the King, the
Buddha, and the Queen, this sutra. Even though they have
not yet attained the supreme truth and so cannot yet expound
it, they should still be universally respected as great
Bodhisattvas.

5. The Marvelous Power of the Dragon's Children.

According to legend, a dragon's children can produce
clouds and rain seven days after their birth. Likewise, those
who practice this sutra, even though they are still tainted with
selfish desires, can demonstrate the way of great Bodhisattvas. They can make a day extend to one hundred *kalpas*
or reduce the length of a *kalpa* to a day or two. (This suggests
that the term *kalpa*, besides indicating a quantitative length of
time, can also refer to a quality of life. We say that "time flies"
when we are having fun, but "drags" when we suffer pain or
boredom.)

6. The Marvelous Power of Governing Fairly.

Even a young prince can govern his country during his
father's absence. Likewise, those who uphold, read, and recite this sutra can act as the Buddha's emissaries and finally
become Buddhas themselves.

7. The Marvelous Power of Reward.

If a brave soldier performs valiantly in battle, the King might promote him and reward him handsomely. Likewise, the Buddha rewards his valiant followers and promotes them to the seventh grade of Bodhisattva. Those who practice this sutra achieve the rank called Non-retrogression. They will never again slip backwards, but will proceed surely to the highest rank of all, Buddhahood.

8. The Marvelous Power of Endurance.

Those who uphold, read, recite, and spread this sutra to others will be able to propagate it by skillful expedients, purify the Buddha Land, and attain Buddhahood.

9. The Marvelous Power of Salvation.

If people enthusiastically uphold, read, recite, and explain this sutra to others, they will be able to purify themselves and immediately reduce whatever evil karma they have inherited from previous lives. They will also obtain several types of *samadhi* (concentration), such as the *Samadhi of Surangama* (which is explained in the sutra of that name), and save all manner of living beings from sufferings, leading them to emancipation.

10. The Marvelous Power of Ascending.

If people practice this sutra and lead others to practice it, they will yearn to become great Bodhisattvas, ascend through the various ranks of Bodhisattva accomplishments, and finally reach the highest rank, which is called "Dharma Cloud." Out of their compassion for others, they will reach out to them, save them, and finally attain Supreme Enlightenment.

These are the ten merits of Marvelous Power. Great-Adornment Bodhisattva and his companions were delighted to learn them, expressed their appreciation to Sakyamuni Buddha, and vowed to him that they would spread this sutra after he entered into nirvana.

The Sutra of the Lotus Flower of the Wonderful Law

CHAPTER I: INTRODUCTORY

(The First Assembly on Mt. Sacred Eagle)

Chapter One, "Introductory," is the preface of the Lotus Sutra and a prologue to the teachings to be unfolded in the chapters which follow. This chapter opens with the words, 'Thus have I heard." This phrase, which is used to open most sutras, is generally interpreted as, "I have heard in this way." The Lotus Sutra, however, expects us to read it instead as, "I have heard *this.*"

All sutras are records of the teachings of Sakyamuni, which were orally transmitted and then put into writing by various disciples or their successors some years after his death. Therefore, "I" represents the disciple who originally heard this sutra and transmitted it orally before it was set down in writing. Although the author's name is unknown, legend attributes it to Ananda, one of the ten great disciples of Sakyamuni.

"Thus have I heard," literally means, "I have heard the Buddha's teachings in this way." But it also implies that others might have interpreted them in some other way. Sakyamuni employed an expedient method of preaching so that he could be understood by the individual listener in his or her particular situation. For this reason, the interpretations of his teachings varied among the believers. Thus a large number of sutras were created over the years, and they did not always agree in their details. The meaning of the Lotus Sutra, however, cannot be interpreted differently, because, unlike the others, it is not a mere expedient for some listeners only, but the final teaching for everyone. Therefore, this sutra expects us to read the opening words as, "I have heard THIS," emphasizing that everyone surely hears and understands it the same way.

Right after these words, the sutra explains where and when it was preached. "The Buddha once lived on Mt. Grdhrakuta ("Mount Sacred Eagle," in Chinese) near the city of Rajagriha." This was probably the largest city in India at the time. Then comes a description of the multitude of listeners, tens of thousands of beings, human, superhuman, and sub-human (in other words, representatives of all living things), who had gathered to hear the definitive teaching. They are listed as follows:

1. Twelve thousand *arhats* ("worthy ones"), who had attained enlightenment by practicing the teachings of the Lesser Vehicle. Among them were such famous disciples as Maha-Kasyapa, Sariputra, and Maha-Maudgalyayana.

2. Two thousand other disciples, called *sravakas* (hearers), some of whom had something more to learn, while others had nothing more to learn.

3. Sakyamuni's foster-mother Prajapati, and his former wife, Yasodhara, both of whom had become nuns and were accompanied by 6,000 women.

4. Eighty thousand Bodhisattvas, including Manjusri, Avalokitesvara ("World Voice Perceiver"), and Maitreya.

5. Seventy-two thousand denizens of heavenly worlds—that is, angels.

6. Eight "dragon-kings" with hundreds of thousands of attendants.

7. Heavenly musicians called *kimnara*-kings, who were accompanied by numerous attendants.

8. Heavenly musicians called *gandharva*-kings, from the heaven of thirty-three celestial cities. They, too, are accompanied by numerous attendants.

9. Fierce *asura*-kings, spirits of strife and turmoil. They are accompanied by numerous attendants.

10. Winged *garuda*-kings, enemies of the dragons. They are accompanied by numerous attendants.

11. King Ajatasatru, ruler of the country of Magadha (where Mt. Sacred Eagle was located), who had seized the throne by murdering his own father, but had since repented. He, was accompanied by his court.

Besides these mythological creatures, all kinds of human and nonhuman beings assembled around the Buddha to hear his sermon. Although many of them were natural enemies, their harmonious gathering together indicates that the teaching of the Lotus Sutra applies to and unifies all beings.

The congregation waited anxiously for this definitive sermon, the way to which had already been prepared by the Sutra of Innumerable Teachings. But Sakyamuni did not begin immediately. First, he preached the opening sutra, as we saw. Then he entered into its deep meditation. His body and mind became motionless. The assembled gods rained *mandarava* flowers upon him. The world quaked in six ways. The assembled beings looked on in astonishment and joined their hands together in supplication. Finally the Buddha emitted a ray of light from the white curl between his eyebrows (the so-called "third eye") and illuminated all the eighteen thousand worlds to the east, from their lowest hells up to their highest heavens.

These are called the "Six Omens Shown in This World." In order, they are "Preaching," "Entering into Samadhi," "Raining Flowers," "Quaking," "Delighting," and "Emitting a Ray of Light."

The light from the Buddha revealed all kinds of living beings in those other worlds. Among them were *sravakas* ("hearers," that is, disciples of a Buddha) and *pratyeka-Buddhas* (self-instructed sages), who were practicing the Way of the Lesser Vehicle; Bodhisattvas, who were practicing the Way of the Greater Vehicle; laymen and women offering their lives in charity to others; monks and hermits chanting religious texts; others in isolated mountains and valleys engrossed in deep meditation. The congregation could see that each of these other inhabited worlds had its own Buddha, who preached the law far and wide, seeking to deliver people from sufferings. Persons who tried to put their teachings into practice, however, were often having to endure curses and blows from arrogant neighbors.

In the Buddha's light, the congregation could see that some wise people had given up earthly desires, aware that all forms of existence are as insubstantial as the sky. Others made offerings to the relics of the Buddhas or built monuments (stupas) for them. For those in the congregation who could not make out all the details, the Bodhisattva Maitreya, who is to be our next Buddha, recounted everything he saw. The congregation was amazed at these things and thought there must be some explanation for them. Even Maitreya did not know the answer, so he put the question to Manjusri, who was considered the wisest of all the Buddha's disciples, wiser, it was said, than any three men. Manjusri, who had served countless Buddhas in his past lives, replied that he had, indeed, seen this phenomenon before. He said:

> Good men! I think that the Buddha, the World-Honored One, wishes to expound a great teaching, to send the rain of a great teaching, to blow the conch-shell (horn) of a great teaching, to beat the drum of a great teaching, and to explain the meaning of a great teaching.
>
> Good men! I met many Buddhas in my previous existences. At that time, I saw the same good omen as this. Those other Buddhas emitted the same ray of light as this and then ex-

pounded a great teaching. Therefore, know this! I think that this Buddha also is emitting this ray of light and showing this good omen, wishing to cause all living beings to hear and understand the most difficult teaching in all the world to believe.

Then he went on to tell his story, tracing his experience back to previous existences.

Incalculable eons ago, there lived a Buddha called Sun-Moon-Light. He expounded the right teachings to people. To the believers of the three vehicles, hearers, self-taught ones, and Bodhisattvas, he expounded the right teachings in three different ways according to their capacities to understand. After his extinction, there appeared another Buddha with the same name, and after him, yet another and another. Altogether, there were twenty thousand Buddhas named Sun-Moon-Light, one after the other. The last of that name, who had been a king before renouncing the world, had eight sons. When they saw their father abdicate his throne and become a Buddha, these eight sons followed him. They renounced the world, steadfastly performed pure practices, and became teachers of the law.

Meanwhile, the last Sun-Moon-Light Buddha did exactly what the present Buddhas has done. That is, he expounded a sutra of the Great Vehicle called Innumerable Teachings, and then entered into its samadhi. After displaying unusual omens, he emitted a ray of light illuminating all the corners of eighteen thousand Buddha-worlds. Many Bodhisattvas in his congregation were astonished and wanted to know why he had done this. Among them was a Bodhisattva called Varaprabha ("Wonderful-Light"), who had eight hundred disciples. It was to this Bodhisattva and his disciples that the Buddha expounded the Sutra of the Lotus Flower of the Wonderful Law.

The listeners heard the sutra expounded for sixty small *Kalpas*, but they were so enthralled by it that it seemed to last no more than a mealtime. Finishing his preaching, the Buddha announced that at midnight he would enter the nirvana-with-out-remainder (extinction). He assured a Bodhisattva named Srigarbha ("Virtue-Store") that he would soon become a Buddha himself. Then at midnight he expired, just as he had foretold. Afterwards Wonderful-Light led the others in expounding the Lotus Sutra. The eight sons of the Buddha became his disciples and eventually attained Buddhahood (pp. 13-16).

There are two meanings to nirvana. One is the state of enlightenment attained by Sakyamuni after he eliminated all earthly desires. The other is the extinction of a Buddha's body upon the coming of physical death. The idea behind these definitions is that the Buddha attained eternal life with the extinction of his body.

Manjusri then changed his tone of voice and said to Maitreya:

Among the eight hundred disciples of Wonderful-Light Bodhisattva, there was one who did not work very hard. That one was none other than you. I know, because I was Wonderful-Light in my previous life (p. 16).

This is a summary of the first chapter. The reader should bear in mind that at this point Sakyamuni's preaching has not yet begun. In fact, the speakers here are not Sakyamuni but Maitreya and Manjusri, with the former asking the questions and the latter answering them. Sakyamuni takes no part at all in the conversation. His teachings will begin in the next chapter, "Expedients." The two major elements of this chapter are: (1) Maitreya Bodhisattva's description of the scene of various living beings illuminated by the ray of light emitted from the white curl between the Buddha's eyebrows (in the present), and (2) Manjusri's narrative on Wonderful-Light Bodhisattva (in the past). What is the significance of these stories?

First of all, the narrative tells us that the Buddha's light illuminated the east. Is there any special meaning to the east? One interpretation is that illuminating the east actually means illuminating all directions, because the east represents them all. Another idea comes from Sanskrit. As the word *purva* ("east" in Sanskrit) also means "past" or "origin," illuminating the east could be interpreted as "illuminating the origin of humanity." At any rate, the chapter depicts in detail all kinds of spiritual seekers who are illuminated by the ray of light. This symbolizes the universality of the Lotus Sutra, a teaching that is applicable throughout the cosmos.

In addition, Manjusri's narrative on Sun-Moon-Light Buddha illustrates that the Lotus Sutra was expounded in the past just as it is in the present. It is the universal teaching transcending even the concept of time. It is not some recent invention. The subsequent appearance of twenty thousand Buddhas with the same name suggests that the personalities of all Buddhas originate in the spirit of the very first One. Here we get the first glimpse of the "infinite absolute Buddha," or Original Buddha, who will fully reveal himself in Chapter Sixteen, "The Duration of the Life of the Tathagata."

Sun-Moon-Light Buddha expounded the Lotus Sutra prior to entering nirvana, and then assured one of his disciples of his future Buddhahood. The same can be said about Sakyamuni. The Lotus Sutra is the written teachings of Sakyamuni that were expounded prior to his death. In them, he too assured disciples of their future Buddhahood.

Sun-Moon-Light Buddha assigned one of his followers, Wonderful-Light Bodhisattva, to preserve and spread his teachings after he was gone. Likewise, Sakyamuni assigned his followers the task of spreading his teachings in this world after he should enter nirvana. This theme will be developed later, beginning in Chapter Ten, "The Teacher of the Law," and continuing for many chapters after.

Thus this chapter introduces ideas which serve as a prelude to or foreshadowing of the philosophy of the Lotus Sutra, presenting themes which will gradually unfold in the chapters which follow.

The Sutra of the Lotus Flower of the Wonderful Law

CHAPTER II: EXPEDIENTS

(The First Assembly on Mt. Sacred Eagle)

Chapter Two, "Expedients," is one of the most important in the book. It clarifies the fundamental ideas of the "provisional Imprinted Traces," or first half of the sutra. What are these fundamental ideas?

It is widely known that the Lotus Sutra contains the authentic teaching of the Buddha, or the long-awaited final Dharma—the law which underlies all other laws. Prior to the emergence of the Lotus Sutra, a variety of sutras were preached as means or expedients to lead living beings to enlightenment. This chapter also begins with expedients, suggesting that such expedients and the true teaching cannot be separated from each other. They are closely related, and should be considered as parts of one whole.

What is the significance of expedients? First of all, let us think about this question from the standpoint of Buddhism in general.

There is a legend that Sakyamuni, when he attained enlightenment under the Bodhi-tree at Buddha-Gaya, in north-eastern India, was so impressed by its profundity that he remained motionless for hours. Then the Heavenly-King-Brahman, the lord of our world, came to him and said, "Your state of enlightenment is, indeed, impressive. Nevertheless, no matter how wonderful it may be to you, what good is it to anyone else? How are you going to serve people if you remain silent? Now that you have attained the ultimate truth, please expound it to the people of the world and deliver them, too, from suffering." After considering this request, Sakyamuni nodded in agreement, rose from his seat, and set out for Sarnath, where he delivered his first sermon.

This legend shows that the profound depth of the Buddha's enlightenment is almost impossible to express in words. (Otherwise the Buddha would have taught it immediately.) Nevertheless, it must be presented in words and expressed somehow if it is to help people. Words, however, are not always the perfect means of representing facts; they can express only part of them. For instance, we often find it difficult to express our innermost thoughts or complicated physical problems in words. (Physicists generally must resort to mathematical formulae; musicians use music; artists paint, and so on.)

Besides, words function only if commonly understood within a given society. If they are clearly understood, they bear objective meanings. This objectivity, however, is not absolute. It depends on conventional practices mutually agreed upon within a particular society. Something acceptable or commonly understood within one society may be neither acceptable nor understood in another society. Words, by themselves, cannot express the truth in full. If someone wants to expound the truth in words, his explanation will naturally have the characteristic of an expedient. The truth of enlightenment is beyond all our normal experience. There are no words to describe it. Therefore it can be expressed only partially, by expedients. Moreover, each expedient can be presented only in a limited form and on a case-by-case basis. (What makes good sense to one person may make no sense at all to somebody else.)

Sakyamuni had numerous followers and believers. Because their social and educational backgrounds were so diverse, he expounded the law in various ways according to each individual's background. Furthermore, as the level of their understanding also differed, the Buddha adjusted his ways of preaching accordingly. This approach is called the expedient method of teaching. It resulted in a variety of sutras. The teachings in these sutras were not necessarily the same. They were presented as expedients for one single purpose: to lead people to aspire to the same enlightenment as that of the Buddha. Because all of these expedients came out of the Buddha's wisdom and compassion, and were results of his desire to communicate the truth of his enlightenment, their fundamental idea must be one and the same despite their apparent differences.

Notwithstanding the Buddha's efforts, people failed to realize that the expedients they had been taught were only part of the vast and profound truth attained by their master. Gradually they divided into different schools or sects clustered around a particular teaching which they believed to be the ultimate. During his fifty-year teaching Sakyamuni had employed a wide variety of expedients. His disciples, who scattered far and wide, noticed that they had received different teachings. They began to argue among each other about which teachings and practices were the more correct.

To solve these disputes, Sakyamuni introduced the Lotus Sutra—his ultimate teaching. Its first purpose was to break the attachments his disciples had formed to their own particular ideas. That is, Sakyamuni proclaimed that all he had previously taught were only expedients. They were partial truths, not the whole. They were separate "Vehicles." Now they must be unified into One Vehicle, the Buddha Vehicle. This concept of the One Vehicle is the central thought of the Lotus Sutra and the chief idea presented in this chapter.

Most modern Buddhist scholars believe that the Lotus Sutra was compiled about 500 years after Sakyamuni's death—that is, during the first century of our era. (It was not composed all at once. Some parts are considered older than others.) In the light of this historical assessment, we can deduce that the Lotus Sutra constituted an effort to unify the diverse Buddhist schools of thought and practice which had already developed. No matter when the sutra was actually written, however, its doctrine should be understood as conveying universal meaning—the truth which transcends any limits of time or place. The Lotus Sutra embodies thought meant to unify all the Buddhist sects, old and new, regardless of their origin.

Although a more detailed classification is possible, the teachings prior to the Lotus Sutra can be divided roughly into three types, called Vehicles: the *Sravaka* Vehicle of the "hearers," the *Pratyekabuddha* Vehicle of the self-taught, and the *Bodhisattva* or Greater Vehicle. These three vehicles are designed to appeal to three different types of persons.

(1) The term *Sravaka* originally applied to a direct "hearer" or disciple of Sakyamuni. Representatives of this group are superior elders such as Sariputra and Maha-Maudgalyayana. In a broader sense, however, students of other teachers besides Sakyamuni can be called "hearers." As a rule, they are celibate monks who live in groups apart from the rest of society and perform systematic practices and study. (Nichiren pointed out that we all are "hearers" when we become involved in a course of studies. The harder we study, the more we cut ourselves off from outside distractions.)

(2) *Pratyekabuddha* ("private Buddha") has two translations in Japanese: *Dokkaku* and *Engaku*. A *pratyeka-Buddha* seeks enlightenment by and for himself without the guidance of a teacher (*dokkaku*), and/or discovers by himself the inter-connected causes of all things (*engaku*). In India there are many hermits living in seclusion in the mountains and forests, practicing strenuously for their own enlightenment. The ones who have attained a certain degree of enlightenment could be called *Pratyekabuddhas*, "private Buddhas."

Although "hearers" and "private Buddhas" are earnest seekers, they have one critical shortcoming. In pursuing their aim for individual emancipation, they tend to become self-absorbed and neglect the needs of other people. This weakness is the main reason why their teachings are called the "Lesser Vehicle:" they carry the driver but no passengers. (Some Mahayana sutras are extremely critical of them, saying that followers of the Lesser Vehicle cannot possibly attain Buddhahood; they are too self-centered. But the Lotus Sutra, as we shall see, opens the door to persons of all persuasions.)

(3) The Bodhisattva Vehicle: This includes those who seek or already possess the enlightenment of the Buddha. Although they neither enter into nirvana nor attain the ultimate enlightenment of Sakyamuni, Bodhisattvas share his ideal of working in this world for the salvation of others. In contrast to the Lesser Vehicle, the teaching for Bodhisattvas is called the Great Vehicle, for it seeks to guide all living things to enlightenment, just as a large vehicle can carry many passengers besides the driver.

The Lesser Vehicle of the "Sravaka" and "Pratyeka-buddha" drew a sharp line between this world of sufferings and the pure world of spirit. Its followers renounced worldly concerns, devoted their lives to religious austerities, and made every effort to attain absolute tranquillity. This made for a two-dimensional world view, esteeming the pure world of spirit and devaluating the everyday world in which we live.

Bodhisattvas, on the other hand, saw the two worlds as one. they saw this world as the center stage for their religious practice, and preached that spiritual enlightenment must be realized in our life in this world. In short, the Bodhisattva's mission to deliver people from suffering is to be accomplished in this world of sufferings. Anyone can practice the Bodhisattva Way while working in any occupation.

In the realm of the Buddha's enlightenment, everything should be basically equal; there cannot be any discrimination between better and worse. But the "hearers" and "private Buddhas" tend to distinguish their own personal enlightenment from that of Sakyamuni. Consequently, even if they do attain a certain enlightenment of their own, it is not the enlightenment of the Buddha. They do not become Buddhas themselves. Instead they are called *arhats*, perfected ones, and are set apart from the general run of humanity.

The Great Vehicle, on the other hand, teaches that there is only one true and perfect enlightenment, that of the Buddha. Anyone who achieves it becomes a Buddha, too. The Lotus Sutra teaches that everyone—whether they be "hearers," "private Buddhas," or Bodhisattvas—can attain true perfect enlightenment and become Buddhas. This perfect enlightenment of the Buddha is called *anuttara-samyak-sambodhi*.

A key idea of the Lotus Sutra is that the three separate vehicles of "hearers," "private Buddhas," and Bodhisattvas are united in One Vehicle, the Buddha Vehicle.

Let us conclude our introductory remarks at this point and examine the contents of this chapter.

Thereupon the World-honored One emerged from his samadhi and said to Sariputra: "The wisdom of the present Buddhas is profound and immeasurable. The gate to it is difficult to understand and difficult to enter. Their wisdom cannot be understood by any *sravaka* or *Pratyekabuddha*, because the present Buddhas attended on many hundreds of thousands of billions of past Buddhas, and practiced the innumerable teachings of those Buddhas bravely and strenuously to their far-flung fame until they attained the profound Dharma (Law, Truth), which you have never heard before, and became Buddhas; and also because since they became Buddhas they have been expounding the Dharma according to the capacities of all living beings in such various ways that the true purpose of their various teachings is difficult to understand" (p. 23).

These are the opening lines. Since everything from here through to the passage known as the "Ten Suchnesses" is one of the most important sections of the sutra, all Buddhists who follow the Lotus Sutra read this section whenever they perform their daily religious devotions or conduct a memorial service.

In Chapter One, Sakyamuni entered into the samadhi (deep concentration) on the Innumerable Teachings, and his body and mind became motionless. Now at the beginning of this chapter, he emerges quietly from that samadhi and begins to speak to Sariputra, one of his disciples. "The wisdom of the Buddhas," he says, "is profound and immeasurable. Their wisdom cannot be understood by any "hearer" or "private Buddha."

Sakyamuni chose Sariputra deliberately. He was a good example of a "hearer" who had attained the highest rank and become an *arhat*. In addition, he was considered the wisest among the ten great disciples of the Buddha. The Buddha begins his sermon with a gentle but firm criticism of the "hearers" and "private Buddhas." The wisdom of the real Buddhas, he says, is far beyond their comprehension. The disciples must break from any attachment to their own way. Its results are only partial, not complete.

He explains this further. Through innumerable practices in previous existences, he says, the Buddha attained the deepest law underlying all laws, the Dharma which no one had ever heard of before. Since then, he has been expounding it in various ways according to the capacities of living beings. But the true purpose of these teachings is difficult to understand. In order to lead people to the law and save then from suffering, the Buddha had resorted to various expedient teachings: stories of past lives, parables, and similes. The reason for these various teachings was to make the law easier to understand and more congenial to people's likes and dislikes. The law which the Buddha has attained is profound and difficult to understand. Its true nature, the "reality of all things," has been attained only by the Buddhas.

He goes on to name the "reality of all things". . .

in regard to their appearances as such, their natures as such,
their entities as such, their powers as such, their activities as
such, their primary causes as such, their environmental causes
as such, their effects as such, their rewards and retributions as
such, and their equality as such despite these differences.

As it is

These are the "Ten Suchnesses," and form one of the
Buddha's best known teachings. Reality in the "reality of all
things" means "substance" or "existence." According to this
teaching, the true nature of existence (the reality of all things)
can be seen in nine aspects as such: (1) their objective
appearances (attributes), (2) their subjective natures (inner
natures), (3) their entities (forms), (4) their powers (inner
potentials), (5) their functions and activities, (6) their primary
or direct causes, (7) their environmental causes (indirect
causes), (8) their effects upon others, and (9) their rewards
and retributions upon themselves.

This is not a classification of existence, but an illustration
of various viewpoints from which the true nature of existence
may be understood. The viewer is the Buddha, these nine
factors essentially make up a whole as a manifestation of his
wisdom. From the first factor (appearances) through to the
last (rewards and retributions), all are unified as one. Each is
ultimately equal to the others, and so really only one "as
such" exists. This one, the tenth factor, is called the "equality
of the nine factors."

At first glance, the above ten items seem logical and self-
explanatory. Its logic, however, is not easy for ordinary
people to understand. For example, "as such" implies "as it
is," and refers to an ultimate truth which has been grasped
intuitively. It is understood by a religious intuition (called
prajna in Sanskrit) entirely beyond our ordinary way of understanding things as this or that. "As such" also represents
reality or the ultimate truth—the way something really is, not
the way we think it is. These ten perspectives are called the

"Ten Suchnesses." Chih-i of China (538-97) and Nichiren of Japan (1222-82) used them in formulating their philosophical doctrines of "each of the ten realms of existence contains the other nine in itself," and "one thought is the three thousand worlds."

Thus the Buddha confirmed the existence of the highest truth, which can be attained only by a Buddha. The next question is, how does Sakyamuni Buddha expound this highest truth to living beings? That is what Sariputra and the entire congregation wanted to know. Three times Sariputra asked for an explanation, but three times his request was denied. (This is called the "Three Requests and the Three Denials.") Sakyamuni had good reason to refuse Sariputra's requests. The audience, you may recall, was composed mostly of followers of the Lesser Vehicle. These people had spent long years of their lives in rigorous religious exercises and were convinced they had finally arrived at the truth. They were called arhats—perfect ones. Most of them would feel insulted to hear that they had been on the wrong track all this time. It is difficult to be told that one is wrong, especially after having worked so hard and accomplished so much.

Finally, however, Sakyamuni decided to accept the earnest pleas of Sariputra. Before he even began to speak, five thousand monks, nuns, laymen, and women from the congregation stood up and walked out. They were sure that they already knew the highest truth, and saw no need to listen any more. Like religious fanatics everywhere, they were arrogant in their assurance and unwilling to be contradicted or belittled. The Buddha remained silent and made no move to prevent them from leaving. "Let the arrogant ones go!" he told Sariputra. "Listen carefully, and I will explain it to you."

This is traditionally called the "Departure of the Five Thousand Bhikshus (monks)." Why Sakyamuni did not prevent them from departing has been discussed since ancient times. The matter should not be interpreted as a lack of mercy on the part of Sakyamuni; quite the contrary, it shows his

infinite patience and compassion. The teaching of the Lotus
Sutra allows everyone to become a Buddha, even heretics
who oppose the right teaching. Obviously at this point the
five thousand arrogant monks were heretics. They were intentionally presented here to show that even a heretic can be
saved by Sakyamuni's mercy and become a Buddha sooner
or later. (The Buddha does not prevent them at this time so as
not to hurt their feelings; he knows that eventually they will
return. At root, all people are the same, as we saw in the tenth
"Suchness." This identity, which exists along with manifold
differences—as seen in the first nine Suchnesses—is called
the "Void" or "Emptiness" in Buddhist philosophy.)

> The law cannot be understood by reasoning. Only the Bud-
> dhas know the law because the Buddhas, the World-honored
> Ones, appear in the worlds only for one great purpose. . . .
> The Buddhas, the World-honored Ones, appear in the worlds
> in order to cause all living beings to open the gate to the
> insight of the Buddha, and to purify themselves. They appear
> in the worlds in order to show the insight of the Buddha to all
> living beings. They appear in the worlds in order to cause all
> living beings to obtain the insight of the Buddha. They appear
> in the worlds to cause all living beings to enter the Way into
> the insight of the Buddha. Sariputra! This is the one great pur-
> pose for which the Buddhas appear in the worlds (p. 32).

This quotation illustrates one of the most important
teachings of the Lotus Sutra—namely, that the innumerable
Buddhas appear in the worlds for the sole reason or one great
purpose of causing all living beings to *open* the gate to, *show*,
obtain, and *enter* the Way to the insight of the Buddha. Thus,
the one great purpose of the appearance of the Buddhas
turns out to be the teaching of the One Vehicle. As the One
Vehicle is also called the Buddha Vehicle, this teaching is
generally called the One Buddha Vehicle.

The Buddha repeats the same idea to Sariputra in different words:

The Buddhas, the *Tathagatas* ("Ones Thus Come"), teach only Bodhisattvas. All they do is for one purpose, that is, to show the insight of the Buddha to all living beings, and to cause them to obtain the insight of the Buddha. Sariputra, I also expound various teachings to all living beings only for the purpose of revealing the One Buddha Vehicle. There is no other Vehicle, neither a second nor a third (p. 32).

As we can see from the above, the one great purpose for the appearance of the Buddhas is to expound the One Buddha Vehicle. The writer has previously mentioned that the Three Vehicles of *Sravaka*, *Pratyekabuddha*, and *Bodhisattva* are unified by the One Buddha Vehicle, and that theme is now developed in this section. The above words specify that "there is no other Vehicle, neither a second nor a third." This idea is so significant that it is reiterated in the following paragraphs. A couple of examples are:

There is not a second vehicle in the worlds of the ten directions. How can there be a third?

There is no vehicle other than the One Buddha Vehicle (p. 34).

Great Master Chih-i extolled the teaching of the One Vehicle as the unifying principle of Buddhism, presenting it as the doctrine which "opens the Three to reveal the One (Vehicle)" or "encompasses the three with the One." Since the Three Vehicles symbolize all the sects of Buddhism united through this principle, the One Vehicle could also mean the unity of all the religions of the world, non-Buddhist as well as Buddhist.

In reality, however, we all live in a world of relativity. We cannot ignore the fact that different opinions and different understandings of the world have always existed. According to the Lotus Sutra, this diversity of opinions should be appreciated and understood as valid steps we are taking on the road to the human ideal of the ultimate truth and ultimate value. For example, we often see conflicting theories in scientific research programs. Since each theory has good reasons behind it, it may be called a truth at that particular stage. But these various hypotheses must lie within the process leading to that truth.

The Sanskrit word *upaya* ("expedient") conveys the meaning of leading to or approaching the goal. The Three Vehicles are such expedients leading to the goal, the true teaching of the One Buddha Vehicle. Expedients are not just means to an end; they have significance in and of themselves. They are valid steps in the process leading to the truth, the insight of the Buddha. Conversely speaking, the One Buddha Vehicle (the final single truth) is revealed in the form of expedient teachings, valid according to the complexity of our world view. So the sutra says, "The Buddhas divide the One Buddha Vehicle into three as an expedient" (p. 33).

Thus expedients equal the truth in essence. It is not true that "a white lie can be an expedient." A lie, white or black, is not an expedient in the Buddhist sense. An expedient is true within its own context.

Meanwhile, we need a central theme or foundation to unify our many theories of the truth—some theme which has already served us well in the past. So we pick out the one which has been of the most value. In Buddhism, the Bodhisattva Vehicle, or Great Vehicle, has been of the most value. Accordingly, the Great Vehicle has two identities: one which is unified as an expedient, and one which unifies the three expedients as the true teaching. The former is the Great Vehicle, the Bodhisattva Vehicle, in relation to the other two vehicles. The latter is the one which is higher in value and embraces the other two by transcending any contrast between them. In this case, the Bodhisattva Vehicle may be a synonym for the One Buddha Vehicle.

Since the Bodhisattva Vehicle is the basis for the unification of the three vehicles, it follows that the "hearers" and "private Buddhas" are themselves really Bodhisattvas without knowing it. So the Buddha says:

> Sariputra! Some disciples of mine, who think they are *arhats* or *Pratyekabuddhas,* will not be my (true) disciples or (true) *arhats* or (true) *Pratyekabuddhas* if they do not hear or know that the Buddhas . . . teach only Bodhisattvas" (p. 33).

Although the Buddha provided the "hearers," "private Buddhas," and Bodhisattvas with three different ways, the essence of the three identities is Bodhisattvahood. Those who don't realize this fact and hold on to their particular beliefs that they are either *arhats* (perfect ones) or "private Buddhas" (self-enlightened), are neither true *arhats* nor true "private Buddhas." When he is teaching them, the Buddha regards them as being Bodhisattvas. They must be Bodhisattvas at heart even if they are "hearers" or "private Buddhas" in appearance. This is why the sutra says, "The Buddhas teach only Bodhisattvas."

Who are the Bodhisattvas and what is meant by the hearts of Bodhisattvas? *Bodhisattvas* seek to save other people besides themselves, just as the Buddha did. The Bodhisattva heart is the same as the Buddha heart. It does not take much study or diligent practice to know the heart of the Buddha and make it one's own. The Buddha is a symbol of the human ideal. Even an ignorant person can experience the Buddha's heart by dedicating his or her own heart to Him, exalting Him as the ideal, wishing to follow His teachings, believing in and praying to Him, and putting such thoughts into practice to the best of one's ability. It is possible for anyone to experience the heart of the Buddha; that is a way of practice which is open to anyone. For example, someone who is trying to help another person or persons (the Bodhisattva Practice) is already experiencing the Buddha in his heart. Such a potential for realizing Buddhahood in one's heart is something every one of us already possesses by nature. (The Buddha was a human being, and so are we; he achieved Buddhahood, and so can we.) This potential is called the "Buddha-nature."

Toward the end of this chapter, the Buddha expounds a well-known teaching called, "A small good deed leads a person to become a Buddha." This teaching states that whenever someone shows sincere faith in the Buddha by performing a good deed, no matter how tiny it may be, this act sets him on the path to Buddhahood, and he or she is sure to become a Buddha eventually. Even though such a person is not yet a Buddha, he or she is on the way, and deserves respect as a future Buddha.

For example, even a person who has never performed any special practice can become a Buddha simply by making an offering, such as incense, flowers, or the wonderful sounds of music, in front of a stupa (a round dome-shaped shrine) or an image of the Buddha. The sutra repeatedly maintains that such people "have already attained the enlightenment of the Buddha." Furthermore, just entering a shrine only once and reciting, "Namo Buddhaya" (Homage to the Buddha!), or offering a single flower, is enough to enable anyone to become a Buddha. What is more, even a child at play, who pretends to build a stupa by heaping up a pile of sand or dirt, "has already become a Buddha." In the same way, if a child draws a picture of the Buddha on a wall with a stick or the back of his fingernail, and makes a gesture of praying to it, he or she has already become a Buddha (or, as the sutra says again, "has already attained the enlightenment of the Buddha"). (The Buddha is pure good: any act of good on our part, no matter how small or insignificant it may appear to be, puts us in his embrace from which nothing can ever separate us.)

The sutra presents various instances, one by one in order, to show that any small act of good will on our part enables us to become a Buddha. From these concrete examples, we can see that the One Vehicle is the teaching of the Buddha himself—boundless in bounty, pouring forth perfect life in limitless supply, lending a hand to everyone, and leading all of us to his own enlightenment. Finally the sutra adds, "Anyone who even hears the Dharma (law/truth) will not fail to become a Buddha!"

As we saw near the beginning of this chapter, the Buddha appears in the worlds for one great purpose: to cause all living beings to open their eyes, to show them and have them attain the wisdom and insight of a Buddha's enlightenment, and have them enter the path of the insight of a Buddha. We can expect to find more details about this in the coming chapters.

The teaching of the Lotus Sutra, which leads all beings without exception to Buddhahood, is the most highly exalted manifestation of the spirit of the Great Vehicle. It strives to benefit all living beings and leave behind no exceptions. This fundamental principle is clearly expounded in this chapter.

The Sutra of the Lotus Flower of the Wonderful Law

CHAPTER III: A PARABLE

(The First Assembly on Mt. Sacred Eagle)

This chapter is named "A Parable" because it contains a well-known story called, "The Burning House and the Three Carts" or "The Burning House of the Triple World." The Lotus Sutra contains seven parables, commonly called the Seven Great Parables, and this is the first of them.

The first half of the Lotus Sutra ("Shakumon" or the "Theoretical Section") is characterized by three stages of preaching. That is, the same subject is presented in three different ways according to the capacities of the hearers: first by a theory, then by a parable, and finally by means of a story from some previous existence. The teaching of the One Vehicle, for instance, is first presented theoretically in Chapter Two. Then it is illustrated by parables in Chapters Three, Four, Five, and Six. Finally its reason and purpose is clarified in Chapter Seven by a story from a previous existence.

The preceding chapter has revealed the teaching of the One Vehicle, which includes the content of the most profound enlightenment of the Buddha and is the one great purpose for which the Buddhas appear in worlds. Sariputra was delighted to hear this teaching which he had never heard before. According to the opening lines of this chapter:

> Sariputra, who felt like dancing with joy stood up, pressed his palms together, looked up at the honorable face, and said to the Buddha, "Hearing this truthful voice of yours, I feel like dancing with joy. I have never felt like this before" (p. 51).

41

Why was he so delighted? He explains that previously, as one of the "hearers," he had been satisfied with his accomplishments, but couldn't help feeling that he was still missing something. Now at last he understood what had been bothering him, and realized that he was truly a child of the Buddha. In his words:

> Having followed the Buddhas, we have heard the Dharma (law/truth) before. We noticed, however, that the Bodhisattvas were assured of their future Buddhahood, but no such thing ever happened to us. So we deeply regretted that we were not given the immeasurable insight of the Buddha. While I was sitting alone under a tree or wandering about in mountains and forests, I thought to myself, "We hearers entered the same world of the Dharma as the Bodhisattvas did. Why does the Buddha save us only by the teachings of the Lesser Vehicle?" Having heard your words, I now understand that the fault was on our side, not the Buddha's because if we hearers had waited for you to expound the way to complete perfect enlightenment (*anuttara-samyak-sambodhi*), we too would have been saved by the Great Vehicle. When we heard your first teaching, we did not realize that it was only an expedient device in accord with our capacities. Therefore we received and believed that teaching at once, thought it over, and attained its enlightenment. Still I reproached myself day and night. Now I have heard from you the law that I never heard before. I have removed all my doubts. Now I am calm and peaceful in body and mind. Today, I have realized that I am your son, that I was born from your mouth (p. 51-52).

In response, Sakyamuni told him:

> Under two billion Buddhas in the past, I (Sakyamuni) always taught you (Sariputra) in order to cause you to attain unsurpassed enlightenment. You studied under me throughout the long night. I caused you to aspire to the enlightenment of the Buddha (the Great Vehicle) in your previous existence. You

had forgotten all this, and thought that you had already attained extinction. In order to cause you to remember the way
you practiced under your original vow (of the Bodhisattva), I
am now expounding to you "hearers" this sutra of the Great
Vehicle, which is called the "Lotus Flower of the Wonderful
Law," that by which Bodhisattvas are instructed and which is
upheld by all the Buddhas. After a countless, inconceivable
number of eons from now, you will be able to make offerings
to many thousands of billions of Buddhas, keep their right
teachings, practice the way a Bodhisattva should practice, and
become a Buddha to be called Padmaprabha (Flower-Light).
The world of that Buddha will be called "Free-from-taint."

Sariputra was the first among the Ten Great Disciples
and the numerous other "hearers" and *arhats* who were personally assured by Sakyamuni of future Buddhahood. The
congregation rejoiced to see that Sariputra was assured of his
future Buddhahood, took off their outer robes, and offered
them to the Buddha. (The monks, who had practically no
possessions, were offering their only "luxury." Wealthy followers made more costly offerings.) They venerated the
Buddha and exalted him, saying, "The Buddha first turned
the wheel of the law at Varanasi a long time ago. Now he
turns the wheel of the unsurpassed and greatest law."
Sariputra said to the Buddha:

> You have assured me of my future Buddhahood. But these
> other hearers and arhats here think they have attained nirvana
> because they have emancipated themselves from such views
> as "I exist" or "I shall exist forever," or "I shall cease to exist."
> They are now quite perplexed because they have heard from
> you the law which they never heard before. World-honored
> One, in order to free them from their doubts, explain why you
> said all this to them (p. 60).

Thus Sariputra pleaded for his fellow-disciples. In reply,
Sakyamuni said, "I told you that the Buddhas expound the

law with expedients and other means only for the purpose of
causing all living beings to attain supreme-perfect-enlightenment. Let me illustrate this with a parable." Then he told the
parable for which this chapter is named.

Suppose there once lived a very rich man in a certain country. His wealth was vast. He had many rice fields, houses, and
servants. Although his manor house was large, it had only one
gate. Many people lived in that house, as much as five hundred, of whom thirty were his own children. The building was
old and in disrepair, the fences and walls dilapidated, the
bases of the pillars rotten, and the beams and ridgepoles tilt-
ing and slanted. Besides, although people had not noticed,
numerous birds, beasts, and pets were rampant in the house.

One day while the man was out, fires broke out simulta-
neously on all sides of the house, and it began to burn. Inside
the house, the children were so preoccupied with their games
that they never noticed the fires and did not try to get out. The
rich man came home, saw what was happening, and thought,
"The children will die if they remain inside. I have to get them
out quickly by any means, even by force if necessary." He
shouted to them, "Come out right away!" But the children,
who were scattered about the house and engrossed in their
amusements, did not pay any attention to him. They continued playing as if they were in no danger at all.

The rich man realized that he would have to save them by
some expedient. He knew that children are attracted by rare
toys, so he shouted to them, "There are toys out her which
you love. You'll be sorry if you don't come out quickly and
choose the ones you want. There are sheep-carts, deer-carts,
and bullock-carts here outside the house. You can have
whichever one you want if you come out right away!"

Suddenly the children began to listen to their father. They
rushed out of the house, pushing and shoving each other to
be first in line.

Once the rich man saw them all safely outside, he felt relieved. The children said to him, "Give us the carts you prom-

ised us!" Instead of giving them separate presents, the rich man gave each of them an identical bullock-cart, more magnificent than anything they had longed for. It was called the "great white bullock-cart."

The cart was tall, wide, and deep. It was adorned with many treasures, surrounded by railings, and had bells hanging on the four sides. A richly adorned canopy was fixed on top. Garlands of flowers, tied with jeweled ropes, were hanging from the canopy. In the carts, there were quilts spread on one another and a crimson pillow. The cart was yoked to white bullocks. The skin of these bullocks shone brightly; their build was stout and beautiful; their gait was regular. They could run as swift as the wind. Each cart was conducted by attendants. Because the father was so wealthy and loved all his children equally, he gave them only the best—a splendid white bullock cart for each one (pp. 61-63 summarized).

Sakyamuni asked: "Sariputra, do you think that the rich man was guilty of falsehood when he gave his children the sumptuous white bullock-carts instead of the ones they asked for?"

Sariputra answered, "No, World-honored One. The rich man saved his children from the fire and caused them to survive. He should not be accused of falsehood, because the children were, indeed, given their toys, even if these toys were better than they had previously imagined. He used an expedient to save their lives, not a falsehood."

Sakyamuni continued, "It is just as you say. Like the rich man, I am the father of the world. I eliminate fear, grief, ignorance, and darkness. I have supernatural skills and the power of wisdom. Out of my infinite compassion, I never tire of seeking good things for or benefiting living beings. I have appeared in the triple world (the worlds of desire, form, and non-form), which can be likened to the rotten and burning house, in order to save all living beings from the fires of earthly desires, to teach them, and have them attain supreme-perfect-enlightenment. I see that all living beings are burned by the fires of birth, old age, disease, and death. They undergo all sorts of sufferings because of their cravings to enhance their lives. The rich man persuaded his children to come out by first promising them the gifts of three kinds of carts. In the same way, I first led all living beings with the expedient teachings of the Three Vehicles" (pp. 61-66 summarized).

The chapter concludes by repeating the same story in verse.

From the theoretical standpoint, this parable explains the relationship between the Three Vehicles and the One Vehicle. The three toy carts—the sheep-cart, deer-cart, and bullock-cart—respectively represent the *Sravaka*-Vehicle of the "hearers," the *Pratyekabuddha*-Vehicle of the "private Buddhas," and the Bodhisattva-Vehicle of those who serve and enlighten others. The large white bullock cart which is given to each of the children symbolizes the One Buddha Vehicle. The rich man first offered his children three kinds of carts as expedients, but in the end he gave each of them an identical large white bullock-cart. Obviously the Buddha told this parable to illustrate that the One Vehicle is true and the three are mere expedients. The differences between the One Vehicle and the Three Vehicles, which were discussed theoretically in Chapter Two, are now explained in a graphic story that anyone can understand and remember.

Some other points are brought out in this chapter. First, the congregation exalted the Buddha as the one "who turns the wheel of the most wonderful, unsurpassed, and greatest law." To turn the wheel of the law means to expound the Dharma (law/truth). As we mentioned before, a legend says that Sakyamuni remained silent for a long time after he first attained enlightenment. Then Heavenly-King-Brahman appeared before him and implored him to expound his enlightenment and save the people of the world from suffering. The Buddha agreed, got up, and walked from Gaya to the town of Sarnath, outside Varanasi (modern Banares), where he delivered his first sermon. We can understand from this episode that expounding the law is a prerequisite for the Buddha's salvation of all living beings. Of course, no Buddha exists who does not preach at all, and all the sutras are written records of Sakyamuni's teachings. However, a careful examination of various sutras reveals that it is not uncommon for a Bodhisattva or one of his disciples to expound the law on behalf of Sakyamuni.

For instance, The Garland Sutra (*Avatamsaka-sutra*) is believed to delineate the inner state of the Buddha when he first attained enlightenment. (But in this sutra the Buddha speaks not one word.) All sutras of the Great Vehicle (Mahayana) are accounts of the teachings of the Buddha, and all urge living beings to believe him and follow him. In most cases, however, it is a Bodhisattva, such as Manjusri, Samantabhadra (Universal-Sage), and Avalokitesvara (World-Voice-Perceiver), rather than the Buddha himself, who do the speaking and save living beings.

In this sense, the Lotus Sutra is an exception. It clearly stipulates that its preacher is Sakyamuni himself, and gives him the specific role of savior of all living beings. The Buddha saves us by the powers of his wisdom and compassion, and these powers are displayed in his work of preaching.

In this parable, the rich father symbolizes the Buddha, while the children represent all of us living beings. In other words, the relationship between the Buddha and living beings is compared to the relationship of a father and his children. That the father saves his children out of compassion for them implies that the Buddha does the same thing. In short, the parable proclaims the Buddha to be nothing less than the universal Savior.

Buddhism is a philosophical religion, and its core is the concept of the Buddha. Profound studies and observations of the Buddha have been conducted from many different perspectives. For instance, the teaching of Mahayana (the Great Vehicle) unfolds its dominant idea that the Buddha is the eternal, infinite truth itself, because he attained that truth, participates in it, and totally identifies himself with it. The

Buddha, when regarded this way, is called the Dharma-body, Law-body, or Truth-body. Although the Buddha as Truth gives us some idea of the profundity of his existence (all existence, for that matter), this particular concept of the Buddha may seem somewhat distant from the world of our experience. Such a truth can be understood (as Chapter Two states) only by another Buddha. It is not easy for us ordinary people to awaken to transcendent reality. The Buddha as Truth is too abstract for ordinary people to grasp. We need a more concrete identity of the Buddha in order to feel his existence.

This parable presents the Buddha as a concerned parent, and so brings an intimacy into the relationship between the Buddha and us ordinary people. On our part, the Buddha appears like a father to be loved and trusted in faith. On the Buddha's part, living beings like us are his children to be saved with compassion. In all of Buddhist literature, there is no other example quite as vivid as this one in the Lotus Sutra, which presents the Buddha as the Savior of suffering humanity. Here in the Lotus Sutra the Buddha touches our hearts with a clear-cut image of his personality.

According to Nichiren, Sakyamuni, a Buddha whom we should recognize as the Original Buddha, had the three virtues of master, teacher, and parent. The Buddha is our master (whom we should obey), teacher (whose words we should study), and parent (whose concern for us is boundless).

Of course, these three virtues are familiar in our everyday world, where they are recognized as ethical values. But religious philosophy must go deeper. Nichiren's reference to the Buddha with the virtues of master, teacher, and parent are meant to humanize an otherwise abstract Buddha, making him seem more human and less transcendent.

Thus the idea of the three virtues signifies that the Buddha, as the Savior of all people, is not just a principle, but also humane in his grace and compassion, like a parent with his children. This view of the Buddha is based upon the philosophy of the Lotus Sutra.

Another important point of the parable is that we humans are allegorically illustrated as living in a burning house. The burning, of course, symbolizes our suffering. From the Buddhist viewpoint, suffering is an inescapable fact of life, as illustrated in the dictum, "All existence is suffering." Many people think this view is too pessimistic, but that is not the case. The dictum is presented as a bare fact, neither good or bad. Biological suffering is a part of life. The question is, What can we do about it?

We have desires as long as we live. Even if we satisfy one desire, another immediately arises to succeed it. As a result, we are always unsatisfied and even frustrated. Besides, to satisfy any desire we must make an effort; we cannot get anything by remaining idle. Thus, whether we act or just sit and dream, we are always unsatisfied. Although there are physical sufferings, such as illness or poverty, suffering in essence may be psychological. (What matters is not the problems of life but how we react to them.) We suffer dissatisfaction as long as we are seeking fulfillment in life. Even striving in the pursuit of happiness means we have not yet achieved the happiness we desire. For this reason, "All existence is suffering" is not a pessimistic view of life. Rather, it can be the reverse image of a positive view—striving to live a better life.

Then why do we end up suffering while pursuing happiness? That is a fundamental question.

The answer is that ordinary people think of happiness as the satisfaction of worldly desires, seeing their lives only from a biological viewpoint. If perfection of our biological lives is our only desire and goal, this world quickly becomes a battlefield of clashing egos, all struggling for survival. Each person pursues his own interests at the expense of the others. In order to achieve true happiness, we must break out of our selfish limitations somehow and find a path which transcends biological existence.

We must first realize that true happiness cannot be the satisfaction of our desires by winning the battle for survival (which is impossible), but rather the establishment of a world without conflicts, where each individual considers the happiness and interests of others to be the same as his own. This is the Buddha's "Pure World." (In it, the Buddha is at the center, not I or anyone else.) Its realization is the only path for overcoming sufferings.

Sakyamuni indicates the path to true happiness by first pointing out that suffering in this world surely exists. Then in the last verses of this chapter he gives the remedy.

> I am the father of this world, the best of the sages. All living beings are my children. They are deeply attached to the pleasures of the world. They lack wisdom. The triple world is not peaceful. It is like the burning house. It is full of sufferings. It is dreadful. There are always the sufferings of birth, old age, disease, and death. They are like flames raging endlessly. I have already left the burning house of the triple world. I am tranquil and peaceful in a bower in the forest. This triple world is my property. All living beings in it are my children. There are many sufferings in this world. Only I can save all living beings (pp. 75-76).

It is based on this passage that Nichiren formulated his doctrine of the three virtues of the Buddha: he is our master, our teacher, and our parent.

The Sutra of the Lotus Flower of the Wonderful Law

CHAPTER IV: UNDERSTANDING BY FAITH

(The First Assembly on Mt. Sacred Eagle)

In the preceding chapters One and Two, Sakyamuni firmly declared that the true teaching of the Buddha is the One Vehicle of the Lotus Sutra. He urged us to believe and accept it from the bottom of our hearts. In this chapter, he unveils how we can believe, accept, and understand it properly. In the previous chapters, Sariputra had been the principal direct listener to Sakyamuni's preaching. Here his place is taken by four other important "hearers." They are Subhuti, Maha-Katyayana, Maha-Kasyapa, and Maha-Maudgalyayana. [Maha means "great" in Sanskrit.]

At the beginning of the chapter, these four disciples express their excitement over what they have been hearing. They wanted to dance for joy when they heard the parable of the burning house and learned that their friend Sariputra, a fellow-"hearer," would someday become a buddha. They arose from their seats, adjusted their robes to bare their right shoulders [as a sign of respect], put their right knees on the ground, and joined their palms together before the Buddha, saying:

We, who are senior among the disciples, have now grown old. We did not seek supreme-perfect-enlightenment before, because we believed we had already attained nirvana. You have been expounding the law for a long time now. While we were your pupils, we grew weary and wanted to attain only the passive nirvana of the Lesser Vehicle. We didn't want to

bother with bodhisattva practices—that is, to purify the
Buddha's world and lead all living beings to Buddhahood. But
now we have the greatest joy we ever had. We are delighted
to see a sravaka being assured of future Buddhahood. We
never expected to hear such a wonderful law. We feel as if we
had received innumerable blessings that we had not even
looked for. Permit us to explain our feelings with a parable
(p. 88).

The narrative which is now told by the four sravakas is
called the "Parable of the Rich Man and His Poor Son." As we
can see from what they have said, the Lesser Vehicle which
they had been following stressed escape from this world of
sorrows into a pure world of contemplation. Its concept of
enlightenment was also passive. It concluded that "nothing is
different from anything else," and "there is nothing more to
seek." This view rejected the reality of this world and the
necessity of working to change it. The Great Vehicle, on the
other hand, interpreted the same doctrine [that nothing is
substantial] positively as becoming a buddha in this world
and transforming it into a buddha-world. Enlightenment is to
be achieved within the turmoil of our daily life, not in silent
seclusion. The four "hearers" now realize that they, too, have
obtained the wonderful law of the Great Vehicle and have
departed from the passivity of the Lesser Vehicle. To express
their new understanding, they tell the following parable:

Once upon a time, there lived a poor man who wandered
about the country looking for work. He had long ago forgotten the happy home of his childhood which he had left many
years before. Now every year he grew poorer and more miserable as he drifted aimlessly about, until one day, quite by
accident, he found himself back in the land of his birth. His
father, meanwhile, had grown very rich and now lived in a
magnificent villa, from which he directed his many employees
and business affairs. However, he never forgot his son who
had left home so many years before, and someday he hoped

to find him again. He thought to himself, "I have no heir any more. When I die, all my accumulated wealth will be scattered and lost. I will have enjoyed all my success for nothing."

One day the son, who had been begging from door to door, came to the gate of his father's villa. He peered in but did not recognize the wealthy businessman inside, who was surrounded by employees and servants obeying his instructions. In fact, the sight of his old father frightened him. He thought, "Whoever that man is, he looks too important to bother himself with the likes of me. I had better leave this place before I get into some kind of trouble." He turned and ran away.

(1) The rich man, however, had recognized his son at first sight. When he saw him run away, he immediately told two of his servants, "Go and catch that man! Bring him back here when you've got him!" When the son saw the two servants pursuing him, he was terrified. "Leave me alone!" he cried. "What have I done to you?" He was so frightened that he fainted dead away.

(2) When the rich man saw how low his son had sunk, he realized he could hold him only by using some ruse. "Pour water on him," he told the servants, "and revive him. Then tell him he is free to go. But keep an eye on him and tell me where he has gone." The servants did as they were instructed, and the poor son got up and slipped away, much relieved that he had not been arrested. Once he heard where his son was staying, the father sent two other servants, much shabbier and humbler than the first pair, with instructions to offer the poor son a menial job. The son accepted, happy to get a day's work. In this way, the father kept his son close by doing menial labor day after day. The son, who was pleased to get regular employment, worked hard.

(3) The father secretly watched his son compassionately. One day he removed his fine clothes and disguised himself as a foreman. He approached his son and spoke to him and a friendly manner. "You do good work, boy. It's time you had a better job. I am going to promote you to a task involving more

responsibility. If there is anything you need, just speak to me about it. I am an old man without a son of my own. From now on, I'll be just like a father to you." So the son continued working at the estate, passing gradually from one job to another, always accepting more responsibility as he became ready for it.

(4) One day the father fell ill. He knew that his days were numbered. He called in his son and promoted him to general manager. The son was pleased to accept the position, but still considered himself to be no more than a faithful employee.

(5) He worked conscientiously, and soon was known far and wide for his honesty and dedication. When the father was on his deathbed, he called together all his relatives, associates, and employees. Then in front of everyone, he revealed his son's true identity and announced that he was the true heir to all his estates and businesses. The son was astonished to hear this. "I never dreamed that I was the rightful heir to all this," he said. "It has come to me totally unexpectedly" (pp. 89-92, summarized).

"World-Honored One," continued the narrators, "the great rich man in this parable is you. We are like the poor son, because we have always been your children without knowing it. We did not know your heart. We clung to the teachings of the Lesser Vehicle. Previously we had suffered as we wandered in the world of birth and death. Therefore you accepted us among your disciples, and as an expedient you taught us the Lesser Vehicle. We felt satisfied when we attained it, and we never tried to seek the Great Vehicle. Although we did not seek it, the Great Vehicle has now been given to us as a free gift, and we have already obtained the fruits of the unsurpassed enlightenment. Now we can be called "hearers" in the real sense of the word" (p. 92-93).

This is a summary of Chapter Four. But why is it called, "Understanding by Faith?" This refers to the mental attitude of accepting faith. Faith appears in an honest heart. Neither logic nor reason can awaken faith in us. Faith grows beyond reason when we encounter someone beyond our capacities, or when we unexpectedly touch something absolute in our lives or in the cosmos. In Chapter Three, the sutra maintains, "They will be able to follow this sutra only because they believe my words, not because of their own wisdom" (p. 80).

We can come to faith only by encountering the absolute Buddha and believing his words. This is an act beyond the working of our knowledge. In Chapter Two, the Buddha says, "Sariputra, know this! The Buddhas do not speak differently." The Buddhas speak truth. We can recognize that truth even when it is beyond our full understanding.

On the other hand, this does not mean that we should believe blindly. There is a Japanese saying that "even the head of a sardine seems blessed if you have faith in it." This is not what we mean by faith. We can maintain a belief that is inspired by the experience of something beyond our ordinary capacities. We can evaluate it by means of our intellect and reason, and form our own mental attitudes. The title of this chapter, "Understanding by Faith," refers to this process of the formation of our own psychological attitudes.

Mental attitudes can be right or wrong; they can be noble or base. Faith that is formed through wrong mental attitudes is nothing more than superstition. Of course, there cannot be any errors in Sakyamuni's teachings. But he expounded the law expediently in different ways according to our needs and abilities to understand. In this parable, the son, who believes himself to be base and humble, is a representation of all living beings. The father (the Buddha) educated his son with expedients in an effort to raise his base mind and make it into a noble one. This superior, noble mind is what we call the heart of the Buddha. Under the guidance of our father (the Buddha), we are all enabled to develop the heart of the Buddha, which every one of us already possesses by nature.

The numbers marked at the head of each passage above show how the son improved his mental attitude by stages. As Great Master Chih-i put it, the parable illustrates how

Sakyamuni presented the truth in stages, giving us (1) the Garland Sutra [Avatamsaka-sutra, wherein the Buddha's enlightenment is seen as too dazzling for most people to understand], (2) the Agama sutras of the Lesser Vehicle, wherein we enter the path of labor and discipline, (3) expanded sutras according to people's capacities [Vaipulya], (4) the Wisdom sutras [Prajna-paramita], and finally (5) the Lotus Sutra which makes us all children and heirs of the Buddha. Buddhism as a whole consists of these five stages of teachings. It could be said that the son's fainting dead away upon first seeing his wealthy father suggests the ignorance of the "hearers," who, according to the Garland Sutra, were unable to appreciate this highest and most difficult teaching among the five.

TEACHING
PATH

STAGES

The Sutra of the Lotus Flower of the Wonderful Law

CHAPTER V: THE SIMILE OF HERBS

(The First Assembly on Mt. Sacred Eagle)

This chapter opens with Sakyamuni praising the four great "hearers" who told the parable of the rich man and his poor son. By their story, they demonstrated that they understood what the Buddha had been teaching. The Buddha said:

> Excellent, excellent! You spoke very well about my true merits. They are just as you said. They are innumerable, asamkhya. You could not describe them all even if you tried for many hundreds of millions of eons. I am the King of the Law. I expound all teachings expediently by my wisdom in order to lead all living beings to the stage of knowing all things. I know how far a living being can be led by a particular teaching, and what each living being has deep in his mind (in his subconscious). Nothing hinders me from knowing all this. I know all things clearly, and show my knowledge of all things to all living beings (p. 105).

Sakyamuni then told them the following simile, which is called the "Simile of Herbs" or the "Three Blades of Grass and the Two Trees:"

> Suppose the various trees and grasses of the one thousand million Sumeru-worlds (worlds containing living beings), including herbs growing in the thickets, forests, mountains, ravines, and valleys, on the ground and by rivers—all these plants being different in names and forms—were covered

with a dark cloud, and then watered by a rainfall at the same time. The small, middle, and large roots, stems, branches, and leaves of the trees and grasses, including herbs growing in thickets and forests, were watered. So were the tall and short trees, whether they were superior in size, middle, or inferior. Those plants were given more or less water by the same rain from the same cloud, and grew differently according to their species. They produced different flowers and fruits even though they grew from the same soil and received water from the same rain.

Maha-Kasyapa, know this! I, the Buddha, am like the cloud. I have appeared in this world just as the large cloud rose. With resounding tones, I expounded the law to gods, men, and asuras (demonic beings) of the world, just as the large cloud covered all the one thousand million Sumeru-worlds. I said to the great multitude, "I am the One Thus Come, the Buddha, the World-honored One. I will cause all living beings to cross (the ocean of birth and death) if they have not yet done so. I will cause them to emancipate themselves from suffering if they have not yet done so. I will cause them to attain nirvana if they have not yet done so. I will cause them to have peace of mind if they have not yet done so. I know their present lives as they are and also their future lives as they will be. I know all. I see all. I know the Way. I have opened the Way. I will expound the Way.

Having seen many thousands of billions of people who came to hear the law, the Buddha knows which ones were clever, which were dull, which were diligent, and which were lazy. Therefore the Buddha expounded to them an innumerable variety of teachings according to their capacities, just like the large cloud caused a rainfall that watered the various trees and grasses at the same time. The various teachings the Buddha expounded were of the same content, of the same taste, but people did not realize it because they were expounded in different ways according to the various stages of enlightenment they were in. Only the Buddha knew that, and led them to attain the final stage of enlightenment. . . . (p. 105-7)

I see all living beings equally. I have no partiality for them. For me, there is no 'this one' or 'that one.' I transcend love and hatred. I am attached to nothing. I am hindered by nothing. I always expound the law to all living beings equally. I expound it to many just as I do to one. . . .

Although my teachings are of the same content to anyone just as the rain is of the same taste to all, so the hearers receive my teachings differently according to their capacities, just as the plants receive different amounts of rain water (pp. 111-113, summarized).

This simile depicts the universal quality of the Buddha, who is like a large cloud that covers all the diverse beings of this world. Chapters Two and Three have introduced the teachings of the One Vehicle (the Truth), which unifies all kinds of philosophies and religions. The One Vehicle can also be understood as a manifestation of the Buddha's personality, because he attained the Truth and manifested it in his very body. In the "Simile of Herbs," the personality of the Buddha, the One Thus Come (Tathagata, the title by which he described himself after his enlightenment), is symbolized by the same kind of cloud, of rain, of content, or of taste.

These allegorical descriptions can be understood as the development of the concept of the One Vehicle. Chapter Four described how the Buddha leads all beings by faith until they reach the final stage of enlightenment. This chapter, on the other hand, tells us that living beings are now at various levels of understanding, and the Buddha patiently and compassionately expounds the law to all of them equally, although in different ways. Traditionally, the small herbs are interpreted as humans and deities, the middle-sized herbs as "hearers" and "private Buddhas," and the large herbs, stems, and branches as Bodhisattvas. The latter can be divided into three levels of accomplishment. The vast compassion of Sakyamuni is distributed equally to all living beings in order to lead them all to the enlightenment of the Buddha.

Toward the end of the chapter, the Buddha assures the four great disciples in front of everyone of their future enlightenment. The details of the Buddha's assurances will be described in the next chapter.

Thus Chapters Three, Four, and Five each introduce a parable. The sutra was arranged in such a way that we can easily understand the theories, which were first introduced in Chapter Two, by means of the parables in the next three chapters. By the end of this chapter, the five "hearers" (Sariputra, Subhuti, Maha-Katyayana, Maha-Kasyapa, and Maha-Maudgalyayana) have been assured by Sakyamuni of their future Buddhahood. As we shall see in the chapters which follow, the sutra will gradually disclose how not just some, but all of the "hearers" are assured of becoming Buddhas in the future.

The Sutra of the Lotus Flower of the Wonderful Law

CHAPTER VI: ASSURANCE OF FUTURE BUDDHAHOOD

(*The First Assembly on Mt. Sacred Eagle*)

It says in Chapter Five, the "Simile of the Herbs," that all the many varieties of sentient beings receive the rainfall of the Buddha's compassion to attain Buddhahood. This means that anyone can become a Buddha. According to his teachings in the Lotus Sutra, he aimed at leading his disciples from the Lesser Vehicle to the attainment of Buddhahood, just like the proponents of the Greater Vehicle. Then, in the final verse of the "Simile of Herbs," he said:

> You, hearers, have not yet attained true extinction. But now you are practicing the way of Bodhisattvas. Continue to study and practice, and you, too, will become Buddhas (p. 114).

When the disciples—that is, Buddhists of the Lesser Vehicle—attain their enlightenment and reach extinction (nirvana), they leave the world and enter a state of blissful liberation. But Bodhisattvas never leave the world. They remain here in this world of ours, with all its evils and sufferings, and even help "hearers" save themselves from sufferings, too. Therefore they don't aim merely at entering into extinction (nirvana) by themselves. (They want all beings to enjoy the same happiness.) The "hearers," on their part, by listening to and accepting the Lotus Sutra, have now begun to share in its spirit, the spirit of Bodhisattvas. They, too, will now remain in the world, keep practicing the Bodhisattva Way, and finally

become Buddhas. The Buddha tells them that this world is
where they will attain "true" extinction.

In this chapter, Sakyamuni assures his four disciples
(Subhuti, Kasyapa, Maudgalyayana, and Katyayana) of their
future Buddhahood, saying that each of them will certainly
become a Buddha in the future. This is called the "Assurance
of the Future Attainment of Buddhahood," which is the name
of the chapter.

The first to be assured was Maha- (Great) Kasyapa:

This Great Kasyapa, a disciple of mine, will see three hundred
billion Buddhas in the future. After making offerings to all of
them and practicing unsurpassed wisdom, he will become a
Buddha called Light, the One Thus Come (Tathagata). His
world will be called Light-Virtue; his eon, Great-Adornment.
His world will not be defiled with slag, rubble, thorns, or filth.
The ground will be even and made of lapis lazuli. Jeweled
trees will stand in lines, and the roads will be marked off by
golden ropes. Jeweled flowers will be strewn all over the
ground, and the earth will be pure. Many hundreds of thousands of millions of Bodhisattvas and innumerable "hearers"
will live in that world. They will protect the teachings of the
Buddha and do no evil (p. 115).

When Sakyamuni said this, the other three disciples
trembled with excitement, looked resolutely at Sakyamuni,
and beseeched him together:

World-honored One! Bestow your words upon us out of your
compassion for us! If you can see what is deep in our hearts,
and assure us of our future Buddhahood, we shall feel as cool
and refreshed as if we were sprinkled with nectar. Suppose a
man should come from some distant country which was suffering from famine. Although he sees a banquet spread for a
great king, he is afraid to partake of it, himself. You, great
hero and World-honored One, give peace to all the people of
the world. If you assure us of our future Buddhahood, we

shall feel like that man being permitted to eat the meal he sees
set before him (pp. 117-18).

Sakyamuni, understanding the wishes of these great
disciples, turned to all the assembled monks and said to
them:

Listen, monks! In his future life, this Subhuti will see three
hundred billion nayutas of Buddhas, make offerings to them,
complete the Way of Bodhisattvas, and become a Buddha
called Beautiful Form, the One Thus Come (Tathagata). His
eon will be called Having Treasures; and his world, Treasure-
born. The ground (of his world) will be entirely even, made of
crystal, and adorned with jeweled trees. Precious flowers will
cover the ground to purify it. The people of that world will
live in jeweled abodes. His sravaka disciples and Bodhisattvas will number in the thousands of billions of nayutas. He
will dwell in the sky (above his world), expound the law to
the multitudes, and save them all equally (pp. 118-9).

Then Sakyamuni continued by assuring Great Katyayana:

This Great Katyayana will make offerings to eight hundred
thousand million Buddhas in the future. After the extinction of
each of those Buddhas, he will erect stupas (domed mausole-
ums) for them. He will adorn them with the seven treasures
(gold, silver, lapis lazuli, shell, agate, pearl, and ruby), make
offerings to those Buddhas, complete the Way of Bodhisattvas, and become a Buddha called Jambunada-Gold-Light.
The ground (of his world) will be entirely even, made of crystal, and adorned with jeweled trees. Only deities and human
beings will live in his world. The four evil regions of hell,
hungry spirits, animals, and demons (asuras) will not exist in
that world (p. 121).

Lastly, Sakyamuni assured Great Maudgalyayana of his future:

This Great Maudgalyayana will make offerings to many Buddhas. After the extinction of each of them, he also will erect
stupas for them adorned with the seven treasures. After that,
he will make the same offerings to two hundred million more
Buddhas. Finally he will become a Buddha himself, and will
be called Tamalapattra-candana-Fragrance, the One Thus
Come (Tathagata). His eon will be called Joy, and his world,
Mental-Happiness. Its land will be a glorious Pure Land, just
as in the cases of the other disciples. That Buddha will continuously expound the law to countless deities, human beings, Bodhisattvas, and sravakas (pp. 122-3).

Thus Sakyamuni predicted the enlightenment of the four
great disciples just as he had with Sariputra. Chapters Three
("A Parable"), Four ("Understanding by Faith"), and Five
("The Simile of Herbs") had used parables to clarify the basic
lesson from Chapter Two ("Expedients")—namely, all teachings are only expedients leading to the One Buddha Vehicle.
The parables were followed up with assurances of future
Buddhahood. In the next chapter, "The Parable of the Magic
City," he employs a different teaching method, showing how
events in the remote past can effect the present and the future. This is called teaching by affinities with the past. These
three methods—doctrinal teaching, parables, and affinities—
are known as the Three Stages of Preaching. All three are
designed to make the basic lesson easy for us to understand.

The Sutra of the Lotus Flower of the Wonderful Law

CHAPTER VII: THE PARABLE OF THE MAGIC CITY

(The First Assembly on Mt. Sacred Eagle)

This chapter has two distinct parts. The first is a story of the previous existence of a Buddha called Great-Universally-Excelling-Wisdom. The second consists of the parable for which this chapter is named, "The Magic City." The concept of previous existences is a fundamental teaching in Buddhism. Its rationale is that there must be some prior meaning or conditions before something else can come into existence. (Nothing comes from nothing, and nothing takes place without a cause.) The story of a previous life here refers to a particular incident in the past which has led to the emergence of a present situation—that is, the origin of things. In the Lotus Sutra, Sakyamuni is said to employ three methods of expounding the law: logical explanations, parables, and stories of previous lives.

The following is a summary of the first part of this chapter, the previous life of Great-Universally-Excelling-Wisdom.

A long, long time ago, there lived a Buddha called Great-Universally-Excelling-Wisdom. His world was called Well-Composed. He lived so long ago that numbers cannot express it. Therefore Sakyamuni explained it by a simile:

Suppose someone were to smash all the earth-particles of one thousand million Sumeru-worlds into ink-powder. Then he went eastward, and with this ink-powder, inked a dot as small as a particle of dust on a world located at a distance of one

65

thousand worlds from his world. Then he continued his journey eastward, inking one dot on the world at every interval of
one thousand worlds until his ink-powder was exhausted.
You could not count the number of worlds he passed
through, could you? Now, suppose all the worlds he passed
through were also smashed to dust. The number of eons
which have elapsed since that Buddha passed away is many
hundreds of thousands of billions of asamkhyas larger than
the number of the particles of dust thus produced. Yet by my
power of insight, I remember that Buddha as vividly as if he
had passed away today (pp. 126-7).

This depiction is called the "three thousand dust-atom
eons." Great-Universally-Excelling-Wisdom Buddha was
once a king, but he renounced the world, performed difficult
practices, and became a Buddha just as Sakyamuni did. The
sutra picks up the story of this Buddha just before he attained
enlightenment.

He sat cross-legged under the Bodhi-tree (tree of enlightenment) without moving his mind or body for ten small eons,
yet the law of the Buddhas did not come into his mind. Then
the trayastrimsa gods prepared for him a lion-like seat one
yojana high under the Bodhi-tree so that there he might be
able to attain supreme-perfect-enlightenment (anuttara-
samyak-sambodhi). When he sat on that seat, the Brahman
heavenly-kings rained celestial flowers, beat heavenly drums,
and made sublime music in his honor. Under these circumstances, the law of the Buddhas finally entered his mind, and
he attained supreme-perfect-enlightenment.
This Buddha had sixteen sons before he renounced the
world. When the sons heard that their father had attained supreme-perfect-enlightenment, they were so pleased that they,
too, left home and family, and went to that Buddha to become
his disciples. In addition, numerous ministers, attendants, and
subjects gathered around these princes and followed them to
the place of enlightenment. There the sixteen princes begged

the Buddha to "turn the Wheel of the Law" (expound the sublime truth) and give grace and peace to all suffering living beings.

When Great-Universally-Excelling-Wisdom Buddha attained enlightenment, five hundred billion Buddha-worlds in each of the ten quarters (of space) quaked, and all those worlds, as well as dark places between the worlds, where rays of light never penetrated, were brilliantly illumined, and the living beings of those worlds were enabled to see each other for the first time. The palaces of the gods of those worlds, including the palaces of the Brahmans, were also illumined by the rays of light, which were twice as bright as those normally emitted by those gods. Astonished, the Brahman heavenly-kings consulted each other and asked the reason, saying, "This has never happened before. Is there any reason for it now? Has a Buddha appeared in the world?"

One of the heavenly-kings led the others westward (in search of the new Buddha). They bore heavenly flowers on trays, and brought their palaces with them. Reaching the world called Well-Composed, they saw the sixteen princes beseeching Great-Universally-Excelling-Wisdom Buddha to turn the wheel of the law now that he had attained enlightenment under the Bodhi-tree (pp. 128-132).

The sutra says that all of the Brahman heavenly-kings from each of the ten quarters came to Great-Universally-Excelling-Wisdom Buddha one after the other. They brought with them their retinues and palaces, arriving like small scattered clouds into one place, transforming into one enormous cloud of spectacular brilliance. They rotated around the Buddha, bowed before him, and rained flowers upon him. The strewn flowers were heaped as high as Mt. Sumeru (the inhabited world). They rained flowers upon the yojana-high Bodhi-tree, too. Then they offered their palaces to the Buddha, saying, "We offer you these palaces. Receive them and bless us by your compassion for us! Turn the Wheel of the Law and save all living beings!"

The Brahman heavenly-kings were unanimous in praising the Buddha and offering him their most cherished possessions. Each praised the Buddha in his own way. The words
spoken by one deity, who had come from the worlds below,
are often quoted:

> May the merits we have accumulated by this offering be dis-
> tributed among all living beings, and may we and all living
> beings together attain the enlightenment of the Buddha!
> (p. 139)

The "merits" spoken of here refer to the benefits they
will receive for offering their palaces. Needless to say, they
also imply merits in general which we all can attain through
our faith in and veneration for the Buddha. The Great Vehicle
teaches that all living beings will attain the enlightenment of
the Buddha, become Buddhas themselves, and be freed from
sufferings. Suppose, however, that someone were to attain
enlightenment, but only for his own sake and not for the sake
of others. This achievement would be in the narrow-minded
and selfish spirit of the Lesser Vehicle. The Great Vehicle, on
the other hand, teaches not individual, but universal salvation: all should equally attain the enlightenment of the Buddha. The words, "May we and all living beings together attain
the enlightenment of the Buddha!" express this merciful
yearning of the Great Vehicle for universal salvation—for the
salvation of all beings without exception.

Kenji Miyazawa, the Japanese poet and author of
children's stories, once said, "Individual happiness is impossible unless the world as a whole becomes happy." The altru-
istic spirit of the Great Vehicle is summarized here in these
words of the Brahman heavenly-king.

Meanwhile, in response to the pleas of the sixteen
princes and the Brahman heavenly-kings, Great-Universally-
Excelling-Wisdom Buddha expounded the teachings of the
Four Noble Truths and the Twelve Interdependent Causes,
which are believed to be the fundamental ideas of Buddhism.

They were expounded mainly for those people who were seeking enlightenment by the Lesser Vehicle.

While Great-Universally-Excelling-Wisdom Buddha was expounding these teachings, all the sixteen princes renounced the world and became sramaneras (novice monks). In time they sought supreme-perfect-enlightenment, and asked the Buddha to explain it to them. Many others did likewise. Then after 20,000 eons, the Buddha expounded the Lotus Sutra. The sixteen princes received it by faith and finally attained what they had sought—supreme-perfect-enlightenment. Great-Universally-Excelling-Wisdom Buddha continued expounding the Lotus Sutra for eight thousand eons. Afterwards, he entered a quiet place and practiced dhyana-concentration for another 84,000 eons. While he was practicing meditation, the sixteen princes, who were now Bodhisattvas, taught the Lotus Sutra and led many people to enlightenment.

After 84,000 eons, Great-Universally-Excelling-Wisdom Buddha emerged from his samadhi (meditation), returned to his dharma-throne (place of teaching), and said to all the people:

> These sixteen sramaneras are Bodhisattvas. Their faculties are sharp and their wisdom is penetrating. In their previous lives, they served many hundreds of thousands of billions of Buddhas, performed brahma practices, and led living beings to enter the worlds of those Buddhas. You should all make offerings to them. Anyone, be they "hearers," "private Buddhas," or Bodhisattvas, if they believe this sutra which has been expounded by the sixteen Bodhisattvas, and keep it, will be able to attain supreme-perfect-enlightenment—that is, the wisdom of the Buddha (p. 142).

This is the narrative of Great-Universally-Excelling-Wisdom Buddha. After telling this story, Sakyamuni discloses that these sixteen Bodhisattva-disciples have already attained enlightenment and are now Buddhas. Their names and locations are: in the east, Aksobhya and Sumeru-Peak; in the

southeast, Lion-Voice and Lion-Form; in the south, Sky-
Dwelling and Eternal-Extinction; in the southwest, Imperial-
Form and Brahma-Form; in the west, Amitayus and Savior-of-
All-Worlds-from-Suffering; in the northwest, Supernatural-
Penetration-of-the-Fragrance-of-Tamalapattra-and-Candana
and Sumeru-Form; in the north, Cloud-Freedom and Cloud-
Freedom-King; in the northeast, He Who Eliminates Fear in
All Worlds; and in the center is Sakyamuni himself. The sutra
also supplies the name of each Buddha's Buddha-world
(ideal world). By listing the names of the Buddhas,
Sakyamuni reveals that in a previous existence, he himself
had been one of those sixteen princes who had become
Bodhisattva-disciples. What is more, he proclaimed that he
was the central Buddha, since he was the sixteenth of those
princes, and the one who was to conclude the story.

The narrative of Great-Universally-Excelling-Wisdom
Buddha can be considered an introduction to the "Realm of
Origin" (Hommon), which is the key philosophy of the Lotus
Sutra. In some ways, this story foreshadows the fundamental
view of the Realm of Origin (Hommon), which will be re-
vealed in later chapters, especially in Chapter Sixteen, "The
Duration of the Life of the Buddha." First, the facts that Great-
Universally-Excelling-Wisdom Buddha expounded the Lotus
Sutra a long time ago, and the sixteen princes kept it and
continue to expound it even now, indicate that the Lotus
Sutra is the eternal truth, transcending the concepts of time
and space. Second, the fact that the Buddhas of the worlds of
the ten directions obtained enlightenment through the Lotus
Sutra suggests that all the teachings of and faith in the Bud-
dhas are to be merged into the teachings of and faith in the
Lotus Sutra. Finally, the central cosmic figure among these
Buddhas is Sakyamuni, who resides in this World of Endurance (Saha-world).

The Great Vehicle teaches us about the appearance of
Buddhas in all of the worlds in the ten directions. When a
Buddha appears in a certain world, that realm is named a
"pure land." For instance, Amitayus Buddha appeared in a

world far to the west of our World of Endurance. His pure land was named Highest Joy or Land of Bliss. The worlds of the ten quarters are called "the other pure lands," since they are on other sides of our World of Endurance. A pure land is an ideal world beyond the concrete reality of our world. But if the notion of pure lands were to ignore this world of ours (the only place of reality), those places would be no more than imaginary existences. The other pure lands would have no entities unless the real World of Endurance existed (that is, unless they originated here in our minds in harmony with the mind of the Buddha). Therefore a true pure land must be realized here where we are.

In the chapters which follow, the Lotus Sutra will affirm that: (1) faith in Sakyamuni Buddha of this our World of Endurance and (2) practices based on that faith should be the core of Buddhism, even though many subsidiary teachings may exist.

Meanwhile, the story of the sixteen princes is intended to teach that the Bodhisattvas (the princes) must do what Sakyamuni did—save all living beings by teaching the truth. Although the profound wisdom of the Buddha is beyond the reach of Bodhisattvas, they nevertheless share the heart of the Buddha. That heart is a commitment to universal salvation— the act of benefiting others. In the chapters which follow, we shall see some examples of such acts performed by some of the Bodhisattvas, and the story of the sixteen princes here serves as an introduction to those practices.

The story of the previous existence of Great-Universally-Excelling-Wisdom Buddha is followed by Sakyamuni's disclosure that the various teachings expounded since he attained enlightenment were really only expedients designed to lead people to the Lotus Sutra. In this connection, the Buddha tells the parable of the magic city, or as it is often called, "A Treasure Palace in a Magic City."

Once upon a time, there was a place containing a magnificent treasure. In order to reach it, people had to travel a dangerous road, five hundred yojanas in length, and cross mountains, valleys, and deserts. There was a guide who knew this road well. He was a wise and clever man. A party of treasure-hunters hired him to lead them to the place where the treasure could be found. They set out with enthusiasm, but the trip turned out to be harder and more dangerous than they had imagined. Most of the party eventually wanted to give up the expedition and return home. "We don't care about the treasure any more," they said. "Let's quit and go back." The leader thought, "They are giving up too easily. If they turn back now, they will have wasted all this effort for nothing. It would be a shame to stop now that we have gone more than half way. I must think of some expedient to encourage them to continue."

He was a wise man who knew how to create illusions. Using his skill, he conjured up an imaginary city on the road ahead. "Look!" he told the travelers. "There is a city ahead of us! I know that you all are tired, but we can enter that city, find safety there, and refresh ourselves before continuing our journey." Delighted with what they saw, the treasure-hunters entered the "city," lay down in shady spots, and rested, feeling themselves secure at last from brigands and wild animals.

When the travelers had rested and partaken of a good meal, the guide made the magic city disappear. "You see," he told them, "this city was only a mirage. But now that you feel rested and stronger, let's continue our journey. We have not much further to go." Encouraged by their leader, the travelers set forth again, helped each other when they encountered difficulties along the way, and finally reached their destination, the treasure site (p. 144-5).

Sakyamuni then explained the parable:

The Buddha knows that living beings are weak and the road to enlightenment is a long one. In order to give people a rest halfway to that final goal, he expediently expounded two kinds of nirvana (for "hearers" and for "private Buddhas") in the Lesser Vehicle. The Lesser Vehicle is like the magic city. It is not the true end. The true goal in the parable was the treasure-site, which symbolizes nirvana by the Great Vehicle (riches for all). The Buddha temporarily expounded the teaching of nirvana by the Lesser Vehicle as a means (expedient) for leading people to nirvana by the Great Vehicle—that is, the One Vehicle. He divided the One Vehicle into three only as an expedient (p. 145).

The "two kinds of nirvana" refer to the enlightenment achieved by sravakas and Pratyekabuddhas under the guidance of the Lesser Vehicle. Because students of the Lesser Vehicle looked upon the world negatively (as something from which to escape), they eventually refused to continue the dangerous and tiresome journey through life. The enlightenment which they attained could be described as "reducing the body to ashes and the mind to annihilation in the great void." But this, said the Buddha, is only an expedient along the journey. It is meant only to keep people from getting attached to physical or mental objects.

We should, however, say something about the Four Noble Truths and the Twelve Interdependent Causes, which were mentioned above.

The First Noble Truth is, "All is suffering." Suffering here refers to the situation in which we cannot meet our desires or wishes. This truth implies that all life is suffering as long as we are dominated by greed, ignorance of the law, and hostility towards others. Our desires can never be fully satisfied.

The Second Noble Truth states, "The cause of sufferings is ignorance." This means that suffering in life is caused by ignorance arising from our instincts, such as thirst, hunger, sex, and fear.

The Third Noble Truth states, "The extinction of ignorance is nirvana." The sravakas took this to mean that ignorance could be extinguished only by quenching human desires.

The Fourth Noble Truth maintains, "The Way to Nirvana is by practicing the Eightfold Path." The Eightfold Path con-

EIGHTFOLD PATH

sists of (1) right views (a correct understanding of the Four
Noble Truths), (2) right thoughts (the ability to reflect on the
Four Truths), (3) right speech (speaking only the truth and
words of kindness), (4) right deeds (proper acts—that is, morality), (5) right livelihood (making a living without harming
others), (6) right effort (or exertion), (7) right memory
(memory of things beneficial to enlightenment), and (8) right
concentration of mind (correct meditation).

12 LINKS

The Twelve Interdependent Causes are: (1) ignorance,
(2) predisposition, (3) consciousness, (4) "name and form"
(an entity of mind and body), (5) the six sense-organs,
(6) contact (touch), (7) sensation, (8) craving, (9) grasping,
(10) existence, (11) birth, and (12) aging and death. (Since
death results in "ignorance," the whole cycle begins all over
again.) Each cause is dependent on its predecessor. For instance, the first cause, ignorance, is the origin of all illusions.
At the same time, it generates the second action of predisposition, which induces the third factor of consciousness (the
first consciousness after conception takes place), which further produces the fourth cause of "name and form," and so
on. Since the world of illusions is gradually formed through
this chain of actions, we will be able to attain enlightenment
by eliminating these causes one by one, starting with the last
cause.

It is generally said that the teaching of the Four Noble
Truths is for sravakas, and that of the Twelve Causes is for
Pratyekabuddhas.

The Sutra of the Lotus Flower of the Wonderful Law

CHAPTER VIII: THE ASSURANCE OF FUTURE BUDDHAHOOD OF THE FIVE HUNDRED DISCIPLES

(The First Assembly on Mt. Sacred Eagle)

Purna is renowned as the best among the Buddha's ten great disciples at preaching the Dharma (law, truth). In this chapter, five hundred arhats, Purna included, are assured of their Buddhahood now that they have heard the Wonderful Law.

Among the great multitude were numerous sravaka-disciples. After hearing the merciful teaching of the Buddha and seeing that Sariputra and four others had been assured of future Buddhahood, Purna, one of the Buddha's disciples, was filled with joy. He arose from his seat, approached Sakyamuni, and bowed his head before the Buddha's feet. Then he looked up at the honorable face (of the Buddha) with unflinching eyes, and thought:

The World-honored One is extraordinary. What he has done is exceptional. By his insight, he has expounded the law with expedients according to the various natures of all living beings of the world, and saved them from sundry attachments. The Buddha's merits are beyond my ability to express. Only the Buddha, the World-honored One, knows the yearning we have deep in our hearts (to become Buddhas).

Reading Purna's mind, Sakyamuni said to everyone present:

Look at Purna! I have always praised him as the most excellent expounder of the law (Dharma). He has championed my teachings vigorously, and helped me spread them. No one excels him in eloquence except the Tathagata (the Buddha) himself. But don't believe that he has helped only me. The truth is, in his previous lives, he served and helped nine thousand million Buddhas propagate their teachings. That is why he is known to be the most excellent expounder of the Dharma. He clearly understood the truth of the void, which was expounded by those Buddhas, and obtained the four kinds of unhindered eloquence. In his previous lives, he also obtained the supernatural powers of a Bodhisattva, although (he did not display them, and instead) he always performed brahma-practices (pure practices). Therefore people assumed he was a "hearer." The truth is he really is a Bodhisattva, although as an expedient he appears to be only a "hearer," hoping in that way to lead people to supreme-perfect-enlightenment. Not only in his previous lives and in the present, but also in the future, he plays a key role as the most brilliant preacher in expounding the right teachings and helping Buddhas spread them and cause living beings to aspire for supreme-perfect-enlightenment. Eventually he himself will be able to become a Buddha. His name will be Brilliance, the Tathagata, and he will preside in a wonderful Buddha-world called Excellent-Purity (p. 153-5).

Among the Buddha's many followers, ten were outstanding. Each was famous for possessing a particular talent which excelled all others. For example, Sariputra was the wisest; Maha-Kasyapa was known for his good practices; Maha-Maudgalyayana was famed for his supernatural powers; Purna was the best preacher, distinguished for his eloquence. This meant that he was more than just a master of rhetoric and silvery words; he could preach with such clarity that through him people could understand the Buddha's deep teachings, and free themselves from sufferings.

"Hearers" of the Lesser Vehicle usually sought as their goal the fulfillment of their own private training. They expected others to imitate the strict practices which they performed, and had little patience with ordinary people caught up in the problems of everyday life.

Purna was an exception. He looked like a sravaka, but he went about preaching the law to common people, and doing so with such eloquence that he was able to cause many of them to aspire to supreme-perfect-enlightenment. Therefore, in reality he was not a sravaka at all, but a Bodhisattva (one who devotes his life to helping others). Any Bodhisattva must also be a preacher (otherwise he cannot help anyone), and that is why a Bodhisattva is called a "teacher of the law." From Chapter Ten on, the Lotus Sutra will clarify the mission of Bodhisattvas. (Here it is only suggested.)

Thus Purna was assured of his future Buddhahood in a realm to be called Excellent-Purity. The sutra gives some details about this pure land, where the inhabitants will know only happiness. "They will feed on two things: delight in the Dharma and delight in dhyana (meditation)" (p. 155).

A good meal is one of life's most delectable joys. A meal also supplies us with physical strength. In the Pure Land, receiving the Dharma (truth) and feeling peace of mind after entering dhyana will be the joy and sustenance of life. In short, the sutra teaches us that the ideal life consists of feeding our hearts just as we feed our bodies.

Sakyamuni repeated in verse what he had said in prose. One stanza reads:

My disciples are performing
The Bodhisattva practices secretly,
Though they show themselves in the forms of sravakas.
They are purifying my world,
Though they pretend to want little
And to shun birth and death.

The lines, "Though they pretend to want little and to shun birth and death," represent sravaka-practices. The world of birth and death refers to this world, where we live with various desires and sufferings. "Hearers" of the Lesser Vehicle

regarded such a world as unclean. They tried to rid themselves, not only of earthly desires, but even of the world itself,
by entering some spiritual world, where they sought an ideal
state of enlightenment. At first glance, this might seem admi-
rable enough. But if they succeeded in cutting themselves off
from the world, it would be impossible for them to save other
creatures from suffering. Although Purna seemed to be performing these sravaka-practices, he was really practicing the
Bodhisattva practice, helping to purify the world of the Buddha—that is, the world in which we live. Sakyamuni's affir-
mation that Purna was secretly performing the Bodhisattva
practice is attributed mainly to his efforts to expound the
Dharma (teachings of the Buddha), in spite of his appearance
of being a sravaka.

In the meantime, twelve hundred arhats (worthy
sravakas who have reached the highest stage) among the
congregation, upon hearing the teaching of Sakyamuni, were
filled with joy such as they had never known before. They
thought, "How glad we shall be if we are assured of our future Buddhahood by the World-honored One just as the
other great disciples were!" Reading their minds, Sakyamuni
said to Maha-Kasyapa:

> Now I will assure these twelve hundred arhats, who are now
> gathered before me, of their future attainment of supreme-
> perfect-enlightenment. Among them, my great disciple
> Kaundinya Bhikshu (monk) will become a Buddha called
> Universal-Brightness, the Tathagata. After his extinction, oth-
> ers of the group will also attain supreme-perfect-enlighten-
> ment one after the other in future worlds, and become Bud-
> dhas also named Universal-Brightness (p. 159).

Thus the Buddha assured the five hundred disciples of
their future Buddhahood, which is why this chapter is titled,
"Assurance of the Five Hundred Disciples." Kaundinya was
one of them. He was one of Sakyamuni's original disciples
who followed him when he first gave up his princely throne

and set forth on the quest for enlightenment. There had been five of them, and together with their master they had performed arduous ascetic practices (practices which Sakyamuni later said were useless). After the Buddha attained enlightenment, these five ascetics became his first disciples.

Others of the five hundred arhats included Uruvilva-Kasyapa, Gaya-Kasyapa, Nadi-Kasyapa, and Aniruddha. The first three arhats were three of the Kasyapa brothers, who had once been leaders of a group of fire-worshippers. It is said that originally these brothers had bitterly opposed Sakyamuni, and had used supernatural powers to discredit him. They were defeated, however, and they together with most of their followers became loyal disciples of the Buddha. Aniruddha, another of the arhats mentioned, was a cousin of Sakyamuni. He was famous for his clairvoyance, the alleged power of seeing beyond the natural range of the senses. It is said that during his early days of severe ascetic practices, he went blind. In place of his natural sight, he developed clairvoyance.

Meanwhile, the five hundred arhats rejoiced at the Buddha's assurance of their future Buddhahood. They rose from their seats, came to the Buddha, and said: "We thought that we had already attained the ultimate enlightenment. Now we know that we were so ignorant that we were satisfied with the wisdom of the Lesser Vehicle, although we should have been seeking the wisdom of the Buddha himself. Permit us to express our gratitude by telling you a parable" (p. 161).

"The Gem Fastened Inside the Garment"
There once lived a poor man who used to drink too much. On one occasion, he visited a wealthy friend, who offered him cup after cup of wine. He enjoyed himself and drank so much that finally he fell sound asleep. His friend had to leave on business. He knew that his poor companion generally lost his wits when drinking, but he felt sorry for him and wanted to help him in some way. So before leaving, he fastened a priceless gem to the garment of the poor man as a gift. Then he

departed, certain that his poor friend would be delighted when he awoke and discovered his new wealth.

But things did not work out as the rich friend had planned. The drunken man finally awoke, but he did not notice the gem which was sewn into his garment. He got up bleary-eyed and went out, believing he possessed no more than a head-ache. He had no home nor steady work to go to, so he wan-dered about from one place to another for many years, living a miserable existence.

One day he ran into his old friend. The friend was shocked by his wretched appearance. "What's wrong with you?" he asked. "I left a priceless gem sewn in your garment that last evening we were together. I expected you to sell it, invest the money in some business, and get on your feet at last. Why didn't you do so?"

The poor man was bewildered. "Gem?" he asked. "What gem?" He felt along the lining of his garment, and was aston-ished to find a precious stone attached to it. He had been a wealthy man all this time without realizing it (p. 161).

The real meaning of this story is spiritual, not financial. By nature, each one of us possesses a gem of priceless value. By simply being alive, we have the same heart and wisdom as the Buddha, but we are not aware of it. (To be enlightened means to wake up and realize who and what we really are.) This gem in everyone's heart is nothing less than the Buddha-nature, the potential to become a Buddha. Because of our ignorance, we are unaware of our Buddha-nature, and fail to make any effort or undertake any practice to develop it. The man in this story who loves to drink signifies ordinary people like us, wasting our lives as if in a drunken fog.

After telling this story, the five hundred sravakas explain that now at last they understand the teachings of the Buddha:

In your previous life, you taught us to aspire for the knowl-edge of all things. But we totally forgot it. We thought that we had attained extinction when we reached arhatship through the teachings of the Lesser Vehicle. We were satisfied with that. Now by your words you have awakened us. We realize that what we had attained was not perfect extinction at all, but a nirvana which you had taught us as an expedient. You reminded us that, in your previous existence, you had already planted the seed of Buddhahood in our hearts. Besides all this, you have now assured us of our future Buddhahood. We feel the greatest joy we have ever known (p. 161-2).

Thus the five hundred express their boundless gratitude. The chapter closes in verse, as they recount their joy in paeans of praise for the Buddha.

The Sutra of the Lotus Flower of the Wonderful Law

CHAPTER IX: THE ASSURANCE OF FUTURE BUDDHAHOOD OF THE SRAVAKAS WHO HAVE SOMETHING MORE TO LEARN AND OF THE SRAVAKAS WHO HAVE NOTHING MORE TO LEARN

(The First Assembly on Mt. Sacred Eagle)

This chapter is a continuation of Chapter Eight. Here the Buddha assures Ananda and Rahula, the two remaining Ten Great Disciples, of their future Buddhahood. At the same time, he assures the other "hearers," both those who had something more to learn and those who had nothing more to learn. This gives the chapter its name. The terms, "those who have something more to learn and those who have nothing more to learn," are used in the Lesser Vehicle to classify stages of accomplishment. In general, those who have reached the first stage of enlightenment beyond that of ordinary people are called sages. Among sages are some who have something more to learn in order to attain perfect enlightenment, and some who require no more training because they have already attained the ultimate truth. The frequently mentioned arhats belong in this category. They have already reached enlightenment (although not the supreme-perfect-enlightenment of the Buddha). In this chapter, two thousand disciples from both categories are assured of their future Buddhahood.

Ananda, the first to be named, was a cousin of Sakyamuni. After Sakyamuni renounced the world, Ananda accompanied him everywhere as his personal attendant. He had an excellent memory; he heard everything the Buddha expounded, and kept it in his mind. Immediately after Sakyamuni's death, his disciples gathered together to recall his teachings. The sutras we now possess are believed to have been recited at that time by Ananda, who had heard them directly from the Buddha. This is why most sutras, including the Lotus Sutra, begin with the words, "Thus have I heard." The "I" here is Ananda, who memorized all the teachings and recited them verbatim.

According to another account, Ananda was son of Dronadama, a younger brother of Suddhodana, father of Sakyamuni and king of Kapilavastu. Ananda's older brother was Devadatta, the infamous villain who plotted against the Buddha and his supporters. The younger brother, on the other hand, was a loyal disciple of the Buddha, and served him all his life. He seems to have been a compassionate person, and there are many stories about his kindness and consideration for others. For instance, it was he who intervened before the Buddha, requesting that Maha-Prajapati (the Buddha's foster-mother) and Yasodhara (the Buddha's wife) be permitted to become disciples. At first the Buddha did not approve of women joining his closely knit group, but somewhat reluctantly he allowed himself to be persuaded by Ananda.

Rahula was the only son born to Sakyamuni and Yasodhara while the Buddha was still a prince living in Kapilavastu. When he renounced the world to seek enlightenment, the prince left them both in the care of his father. After attaining enlightenment some years later and becoming a Buddha, Sakyamuni returned home and preached the Dharma to his family. His wife and son then became his followers.

Meanwhile, this chapter begins with an appeal by Ananda and Rahula for the Buddha's assurance of their future Buddhahood. They approach Sakyamuni, bow before him, and say, "Please assure us of our future Buddhahood! If you assure us of our future attainment of supreme-perfect-enlightenment, it will bring joy not only to us, but to others like us."

Upon hearing this, the two thousand disciples, consisting of those who had something more to learn and those who had nothing more to learn, unanimously rise from their seats, bow before the Buddha, and look up at him, thinking to themselves, "We, too, wish to be assured of our future Buddhahood, just like Ananda and Rahula." Reading their minds, the Buddha says to Ananda, "In your future life, you will become a Buddha called Sovereign-Universal-King-of-Wisdom-of-Seas-and-Mountains, the Tathagata. The world of that Buddha will be called Ever-Raised-Victorious-Banner."

In the congregation, there were eight thousand Bodhisattvas who had just resolved to aspire for supreme-perfect-enlightenment. They thought, "So far as we know, even great Bodhisattvas have never been assured of their future Buddhahood. Why have these 'hearers' been so assured?" Reading their minds, Sakyamuni replied to their unspoken question:

In our previous existence, Ananda and I together dedicated ourselves to the attainment of supreme-perfect-enlightenment under Void-King Buddha. While I concentrated on the attainment of enlightenment, Ananda preferred studying the Dharma. Thanks to my concentration, I have already attained enlightenment, while Ananda has not. Now he keeps the teachings of the Buddha and wishes to keep the store of the teachings of future Buddhas as well, living up to his original vow.

Pleased at hearing this, Ananda said to the Buddha,

You reminded me of the teachings of innumerable Buddhas I heard in my previous lives. Living up to their teachings, I will become the attendant of future Buddhas, and keep their teachings, too (p. 166-7).

Then the Buddha addresses his son Rahula.

You, in your future life, will become a Buddha called the One-Who-Walks-on-Flowers-of-Seven-Jewels, the Tathagata. You will become the eldest son of innumerable Buddhas in your future lives just as you are now mine.

Impressed, the two thousand "hearers" said in verses:

You, World-honored One, are the Light of Wisdom. Hearing from you that we are assured of our future Buddhahood, we are as joyful as if we had been sprinkled with nectar (p. 170).

Here the chapter ends. From Chapters Two through Nine, the Lotus Sutra has presented the renowned disciples of Sakyamuni one after another, and tells us that they are assured of their future Buddhahood. Ananda and Rahula appear in the final scene. Why were they the last? You might think that some special consideration would have been given by the Buddha to his close family relatives. Or perhaps he came to them at the end precisely because they were his relatives and should assume positions of humility. But neither was the case. Special treatment of his relatives, placing them either at the front through favoritism or at the rear through humility, was not Sakyamuni's style. In Buddhism, all beings are equal before the Truth. There is no favoritism.

Through the Buddha's assurance of the "hearers," the Lotus Sutra is asserting that the "hearers" really are Bodhisattvas in essence. Although they appear to perform practices derived from the Lesser Vehicle, in spirit they are Bodhisattvas. (This is a liberal point of view; other sutras from the Great Vehicle are generally very critical of followers of the Lesser Vehicle.) In the preceding chapter, Purna was revealed to be a Bodhisattva, or expounder of the Dharma (teachings of the Buddha), because he taught with such eloquence. This chapter discloses that Ananda and Rahula are exemplars of another aspect of the Bodhisattva spirit. They perpetuate the teachings of the Buddha, and hand them down to future generations. Ananda, as a Bodhisattva, appears in many sutras as a disciple who was commissioned by Sakyamuni to keep his teachings. This suggests that it was Bodhisattvas who were authorized to expound the Dharma.

In addition, the Buddha's parental relationship with Rahula, who is here seen as another Bodhisattva, goes beyond their biological ties, and symbolizes the relationship between the Buddha and all Bodhisattvas. He is the originator of the Dharma; they are his heirs.

Thus the chapter clarifies that all "hearers" (of the Lesser Vehicle) can and should be Bodhisattvas in essence. Based on this premise, Bodhisattvas themselves will make a formal appearance in the following chapters. They will explain in detail that, as the heirs of the Dharma, they should play key roles after the death of Sakyamuni and expound Dharma to all living beings.

This chapter about some of Sakyamuni's relatives introduces the one which follows, in which another of his relatives appears: his cousin Devadatta. But he is a very different sort from Ananda. Devadatta was bitterly jealous of Sakyamuni, deserted his company to found a rival group of his own, and even attempted to murder him.

The Sutra of the Lotus Flower of the Wonderful Law

CHAPTER X: THE TEACHER OF THE DHARMA

(The First Assembly on Mt. Sacred Eagle)

This chapter presents a dramatic development in the teachings of the Lotus Sutra, introducing something which has not yet been seen. Until now, Sakyamuni has addressed only the elders, or "hearers," of the Lesser Vehicle. From this chapter on, Bodhisattvas, the followers of the Great Vehicle, make their appearance, replacing the "hearers," and are addressed directly by the Buddha. Previously he has spoken about them; now he speaks to them. Furthermore, the place where the Sutra is delivered will be changed at the beginning of the next chapter. Up to and including this chapter, the Buddha has been speaking on Mount Sacred Eagle, near the city of Rajagriha. After a mysterious phenomenon takes place at the beginning of Chapter Eleven, and continuing until Chapter Twenty-two, his sermon will be delivered around a treasure tower (stupa) which is hanging in space. Since that part of the sutra is delivered from this new location, the section from Chapters Eleven to Twenty-two is referred to as the "Assembly in Space," or "Assembly in the Sky." The scenes before and after the assembly in the sky are called respectively, the "First Assembly on Mt. Sacred Eagle" and "Second Assembly on Mt. Sacred Eagle."

As the title indicates, the teacher of the Dharma is the theme of this chapter. A teacher of the Dharma is one who expounds or propagates the Dharma (universal law or truth). If Bodhisattvas are expected to expound the Dharma, all of them must already be teachers of the Dharma. Why, then,

89

does the Sutra purposely use the term, "teacher of the
Dharma," instead of simply saying, "Bodhisattva?" As we
mentioned above, it was not until he expounded and propagated the Dharma that Sakyamuni was able to save people. In
other words, Sakyamuni the Savior is nothing less than the
(perfect) teacher of the Dharma. The role of teachers of the
Dharma is to expound the law after the death of Sakyamuni
in order to carry on his saving mission. This and the following
chapters will discuss the practices which these teachers of the
Dharma must undertake.

The chapter opens with Sakyamuni speaking to a
Bodhisattva named Medicine-King in the presence of eighty
thousand great beings:

> Medicine-King! Do you see the many human beings, non-
> human beings, monks, nuns, laymen, and laywomen in this
> congregation, who are seeking the goals for Sravakahood
> and Pratyekabuddhahood or the enlightenment of the Bud-
> dha? If any of them rejoice in my presence, even for one
> moment's thought, at hearing a verse or a phrase of the Lotus
> Sutra, I can assure them all of their future Buddhahood. Even
> after my extinction, if they rejoice for one moment's thought
> at hearing a verse or a phrase of the Lotus Sutra, I can assure
> them all of their future attainment of supreme-perfect-enlight-
> enment. Moreover, if anyone keeps, reads, recites, expounds,
> and copies even a verse or a phrase of the Sutra, and respects
> a scroll of the Sutra just as he respects me, and makes offer-
> ings to it, he or she should be considered to have already
> made offerings to ten billion Buddhas in a previous exist-
> ence, and will surely become a Buddha in a future life
> (p. 171-2).

These words of the Buddha introduce a new development in the teachings of the Lotus Sutra. Up until Chapter
Ten, only "hearers" had been assured of their future Buddhahood. This statement, on the other hand, indicates that not
only the "hearers," but all other people in the congregation

are also assured of future Buddhahood. What is more, the account goes on to say that even after the Buddha's extinction, anyone who rejoices at hearing the Sutra will be assured of his or her future Buddhahood. Furthermore, these words tell us that after the Buddha's extinction, the Lotus Sutra should be written on a scroll, and we should respect it and make offerings to it.

Since the physical body of the Buddha no longer exists after his extinction, the direct object of our worship should then become his teachings, whose substance is preserved in the form of the Sutra or a scroll of the Sutra. The Sutra is the spirit of the Buddha, or another form of his manifestation. If we focus on the time after the Buddha's extinction, the Sutra or a scroll of the Sutra replaces his physical manifestation. In this sense, respecting and making offerings to the Sutra or a scroll of the Sutra is exactly the same as respecting and making offerings to the Buddha himself. Indeed, when we believe, worship, and make offerings to the Lotus Sutra, we in fact believe, worship, and make offerings to the living Buddha. Furthermore, through these practices, we are considered to be worshipping the Original Buddha of Eternal Existence. This chapter and those which follow will gradually clarify what we mean by this.

Sakyamuni's prophetic statements on religious practices in the future, or after his extinction, are the major characteristics of the Lotus Sutra, and cannot be found in any other sutra. In a time when Sakyamuni no longer exists physically, Bodhisattvas are to play the leading role in his place. As we mentioned before, Bodhisattvas have the heart of the Buddha, and their deeds manifest his will. This is why the Lotus Sutra entitles Bodhisattvas to be the teachers of the Dharma. In this sense, Bodhisattvas, or the teachers of the Dharma, can be considered as substitutes for the Buddha. What is more, their role can be considered even more important than that of the Buddha himself after his extinction. Sakyamuni stresses this in his next statement to Bodhisattva Medicine-King:

Medicine-King! If after my extinction, anyone expounds even
a single verse or phrase of this Sutra to even one person, he or
she should be considered to be my messenger, sent by me to
do my work. Needless to say, those who expound the Sutra in
public are also great Bodhisattvas. Even if an evil person
speaks ill of me or slanders me in my presence, he is not as
sinful as the person who reproaches laymen or monks for
reading and reciting the Lotus Sutra (p. 172).

Sakyamuni's words about the teachers of the Dharma
being "messengers of the Buddha" clearly state the significance of their roles. He now goes on to explain this matter in
more detail:

I have expounded many sutras (in the past). I am now expounding this Sutra (in the present). I will also expound many
more sutras (in the future). The total number of these sutras is
countless. This Lotus Sutra is the most difficult of all of them to
understand and believe. This Sutra is the store of the hidden
core of all the Buddhas; it is the greatest sutra ever expounded. Because it is so difficult to understand, many
people despise it even now during my lifetime. Needless to
say, many other people will hate it all the more after my extinction (p. 175-6).

The Lotus Sutra is now declared to be the most profound
of all the sutras. Because of its profundity, it is difficult for
ordinary people to believe and understand. If after the
Buddha's extinction, the teachers of the Dharma expound
this most profound of all sutras, they are sure to be misunderstood and resented. They may even be persecuted by jealous
opponents (for preaching universal salvation and abolishing
distinctions between religions). The Sutra will go on to state
plainly that teachers of the Dharma can expect the worst from
their future audiences. Already a hint of that appears here,
but first the Buddha speaks words of encouragement:

If anyone speaks ill of you, or threatens you with swords, sticks, tile-pieces or stones while you are expounding this Sutra, think of me and be patient! . . . If a teacher of the Dharma expounds this Sutra after my extinction, I will manifest the four kinds of devotees: monks, nuns, and men and women of pure faith, and I will dispatch them to him so that they may make offerings to him and lead many living beings, collecting them to hear the Dharma from him. If he is hated and threatened with swords, sticks, tile-pieces, or stones, I will manifest men and dispatch them to him in order to protect him (p. 179).

If a teacher of the Dharma expounds the Sutra here in this evil world, where the Dharma will be little appreciated after the Buddha's extinction, he might well be persecuted with swords, sticks, tile-pieces, or stones. However, Sakyamuni will create laymen and monks by his supernatural powers, and send them to protect him, although the Buddha himself will not appear.

The teacher of the Dharma will be protected because he is inspired by the power of the Buddha, and his renewed strength can be seen as a manifestation of the Buddha himself. In this respect, the Sutra says, "He (the teacher of the Dharma) will be covered by my robe;" he will be "borne on the Buddha's shoulders," or "reside with the Buddha, who will pat him on his head."

The teacher of the Dharma should expound it with the heart of the Buddha. This idea is presented near the end of the chapter in a doctrine called, "the three rules for teaching the Sutra:"

Medicine-King! How should the good men or women who live after my extinction expound this Sutra of the Lotus Flower of the Wonderful Law to the four kinds of devotees when they wish to do so? They should enter the room of the Buddha (Tathagata), wear the robe of the Buddha, sit on the seat of the Buddha, and then expound this Sutra to the four kinds of followers. To enter the room of the Buddha means to have great compassion towards all living beings. To wear the robe of the Buddha means to be gentle and patient. To sit on the seat of the Buddha means to see the voidness of all things (p. 177).

In sum, the teacher should expound the Dharma in accordance with the three guidelines: (1) the room of the Buddha (which is having great compassion), (2) the robe of the Buddha (which is being gentle and patient), and (3) the seat of the Buddha (which is the voidness of all things). The void in the third rule refers to a mind free from all attachments. This set of three principles, with its clear-cut presentation of the Great Vehicle, is said to be the greatest doctrine of the Buddha.

The Sutra of the Lotus Flower of the Wonderful Law

CHAPTER XI: BEHOLDING THE STUPA OF TREASURES

(The Assembly in the Sky)

This chapter opens with a miraculous phenomenon taking place while Sakyamuni is preaching. The ground suddenly splits open, and a huge stupa (a round dome-shaped shrine), five hundred *yojanas* high and two hundred and fifty *yojanas* wide, springs up from underground and hangs in space before the Buddha. Some say that a *yojana* is about forty miles, and others argue that it is about seventy-five miles (the distance of a one-day trip by bullock cart). At any rate, an enormous stupa—huge beyond our imagination—suddenly appears. It is magnificent in appearance, adorned with jewels and ornaments.

At the sight of this stupa, the assembled congregation bursts into song, offers jewels and flowers before it, venerates it, honors it, and worships it. Then a loud voice of praise is heard from within the stupa:

> Excellent, excellent! You, Sakyamuni, the World-Honored One, have expounded to this great multitude the Sutra of the Lotus Flower of the Wonderful Law, the Teaching of Equality, the Great Wisdom, the Law for Bodhisattvas, the Law Upheld by the Buddhas. What you, Sakyamuni, the World-Honored One, have expounded is all true! (p. 181)

The speaker is a Buddha called Many-Treasures Tathagata ("Thus Come"), who resides within the stupa. Because

95

he proves the authenticity of the Lotus Sutra, which is expounded by Sakyamuni, the World-Honored One, he is
called the Validating Buddha. His stupa is named the Stupa of
Treasures. The assembled people are delighted at hearing
the voice of Many-Treasures Tathagata. They also wonder
how this has happened and what it means. A Bodhisattva-
mahasattva (enlightening great being) named Great-Eloquence asks Sakyamuni about it. Sakyamuni replies:

> The perfect body of a Buddha is in this stupa of treasures.
> That Tathagata is a Buddha named Many-Treasures (Prabhuta-
> ratna), who once lived in a world named Pure-Treasure, lo-
> cated at a great distance to the east. When he was still a
> Bodhisattva, he made a vow. "If anyone expounds the Lotus
> Sutra after I become a Buddha and pass away, I will cause my
> stupa to spring up before him, wherever he may be, so that I
> may be able to prove the authenticity of the Sutra." Now he is
> fulfilling this vow (p. 182).

Much impressed, Great-Eloquence Bodhisattva wants to
see Many-Treasures for himself, and he makes his desire
known to Sakyamuni. The Buddha replies:

> Many-Treasures Buddha made another great vow: "If any
> Buddha wishes to show me to the people when my stupa of
> treasures appears before him so that I may be able to hear the
> Lotus Sutra, all his duplicate Buddhas in the worlds of the ten
> directions must be recalled. Then I will show myself before
> the people."

Then Sakyamuni emitted a ray of light from the white curls
between his eyebrows. The ray of light illumined the east,
where the people saw innumerable Buddhas of innumerable
worlds. Illuminated by the ray of light, those Buddhas of the
worlds of the ten directions came pouring into the World of
Endurance (our world) to make offerings to Sakyamuni Buddha and Many-Treasures Tathagata. At that moment, the

World of Endurance was purified. The ground of the world became lapis lazuli; the roads were marked off by golden ropes; all cities, rushing torrents, and mountains (barriers which divide people from each other) were eliminated. Each of the arriving Buddhas was accompanied by an attending Bodhisattva. They all came to the purified World of Endurance, and sat under jeweled trees on lion-like thrones. All the thrones in the one thousand million Sumeru-worlds (inhabited worlds) were too few to accommodate so many Buddhas, so Sakyamuni purified two hundred billion *nayuta* [one nayuta is one hundred thousand million] other worlds to receive them. Still there was not enough room for them all, so Sakyamuni purified two hundred billion *nayuta* more worlds in eight directions of space to receive them (p. 183-4).

This is called the "triple purification of the worlds." After being seated, each of those Buddhas sends an attendant to pay his respects on his master's behalf, and tell him that his master wishes to see the Stupa of Treasures opened.

In response to their requests, Sakyamuni ascends into the air, and with the fingers of his right hand opens the door of the stupa of treasures. The sound of the opening of the door is said to have been as loud as the removal of the bolt and lock in the gate of a great city. Inside the open stupa, all the congregation now sees Many-Treasures Tathagata, his body intact, sitting in dhyana-concentration (meditation).

Many-Treasures then calls Sakyamuni to join him inside the stupa, offering him half of his seat. Thus Many-Treasures and Sakyamuni sit side by side, sharing the same seat.

Since the seat of the two Buddhas is too high for the congregation to see, Sakyamuni raises them up into the sky by his supernatural powers. Then he says to them, "I shall soon enter into Nirvana. Is there anyone here who is willing to expound the Lotus Sutra in the world after my extinction? I wish to hand it on to someone so that it can be perpetuated" (p. 187).

This statement is followed by verses explaining how difficult it will be to expound the Lotus Sutra after his extinction.

He lists nine examples of unimaginable difficulty, and then stresses in six articles that those hardships are nothing compared to the demanding mission of his followers. The first part of the teaching is as follows:

> It is not difficult to expound all the other sutras, as many as there are sands in the River Ganges. It is not difficult to grasp Mount Sumeru and hurl it to a distance of countless Buddha-worlds. It is not difficult to move a world composed of one thousand million Sumeru-worlds with the tip of a toe and hurl it to another world. It is difficult to expound this Sutra in the evil world after my extinction (p. 190-1).

This is a summary of Chapter Eleven. In this particular chapter, the cosmos is so sublimely depicted that we feel as if we are seeing a drama in space. This majestic picture is a symbolic representation of the ideal world of the Lotus Sutra.

Let us go back for a moment to the Stupa of Treasures. Ordinarily a stupa is a mausoleum where the relics (ashes) of Sakyamuni are enshrined. Once Sakyamuni is extinct, living beings can worship him only in his relics.

The Sutra says that Many-Treasures Buddha will appear whenever and wherever the Lotus Sutra is expounded. This means that the living Sakyamuni, represented by his relics, and the Lotus Sutra are united as one single entity.

Furthermore, Many-Treasures Buddha is said to be a Buddha from the far distant past. Buddhism in general expounds that numerous Buddhas appeared one after the other throughout the ages before Sakyamuni. By presenting Sakyamuni and Many-Treasures Buddha sitting side by side in the Stupa of Treasures, the Sutra implies that the present Buddha (Sakyamuni) and the past Buddha (Many-Treasures) are united as one single entity.

In addition, the Sutra says that innumerable Buddhas or duplicates of Sakyamuni in the worlds of the ten directions were assembled in one place. Each of the duplicates can be seen as a manifestation of Sakyamuni himself, who took the forms of other Buddhas in order to expound the Dharma in other worlds. Now they were all assembled in one place, meaning that all the Buddhas throughout space were unified at that moment by the one Buddha Sakyamuni.

The vast worlds surrounding our World of Endurance are purified three times. By placing the World of Endurance (Saha-world) in the center of those purified worlds, the Sutra shows us that the Buddhist ideal of a pure world must be realized here in our real world, and not somewhere else beyond reality.

Finally, the emergence of a perfect, ideal world is represented by the Stupa of Treasures hanging in space, which now becomes the setting for preaching. The sky in general symbolizes eternity and constancy.

Thus each of the seemingly fantastic events in this chapter has a symbolic meaning of the Buddhist ideal. Based on these ideas, the following chapters will gradually disclose the central thoughts of the Lotus Sutra: (1) the concept of the Original Buddha, and (2) the notion that our World of Endurance is essentially the same as the Pure World.

The Sutra of the Lotus Flower of the Wonderful Law

CHAPTER XII: DEVADATTA

(The Assembly in the Sky)

The Chapter of Devadatta has two major parts. The first half is a story about how the evil-minded Devadatta attains enlightenment in spite of his wickedness, and the second half recounts how the Dragon-King's daughter attains it with the help of the Lotus Sutra.

Devadatta is known as a very bad person. Once he attempted to murder Sakyamuni. It is said that he was the elder brother of Ananda, Sakyamuni's cousin who was the famous reciter of his teachings. This makes Devadatta a close relative of Sakyamuni.

Since childhood, however, Devadatta had been jealous of his extraordinary cousin. After becoming a monk himself, he became arrogant, and plotted to take over the leadership of Sakyamuni's movement. When that failed, he withdrew and started a counter-movement of his own. Finally he decided to murder the Buddha. One day as Sakyamuni was entering the city of Rajagriha, Devadatta let loose in his path a mad elephant, hoping it would trample the Buddha to death. However, a popular story relates that the plan did not work. The elephant terrified people on the streets, and sent them flying in all directions for safety. But when it saw Sakyamuni, it suddenly stopped, and kneeled before him respectfully.

Although Devadatta is known to be an evil person, it is explained here that he had been Sakyamuni's teacher in his previous existence. Sakyamuni describes this to his audience:

PERFECTIONS

A long time ago in my previous existence, I tirelessly
sought the Lotus Sutra. Although I was born a king, I made a
vow to attain the Bodhi (enlightenment) of a Buddha, and I
never faltered in my efforts. I tried to complete the Six Perfections (generosity, morality, patience, zeal, meditation, and
wisdom), and especially practiced the first perfection of generosity. I offered to give away not only my properties, but
even my family, my body, and my very life. Although I ruled
many people in my kingdom, I abdicated the throne, turned
the government over to the crown prince, and left everything
to seek the Dharma. I went about beating a drum and asking
far and wide, "Is there anyone who is willing to expound the
Great Vehicle for me? If there is,—I will become his servant
for the rest of my life."

Then a sage appeared by the name of Ashita, and he said to
me, the King, "I have the teaching of the Great Vehicle, which
is the Sutra of the Lotus Flower of the Wonderful Law. If you
follow me, I will teach it to you."

Hearing this, I danced for joy. Immediately I followed the
sage, offered him whatever services he needed, picked nuts
for him to eat, drew water for him to drink, collected firewood
to warm him in winter, and prepared his meals every day. I
offered him my very body as a seat, and never tired of serving
him. I did all this to attain the Sutra.

The king at that time was I myself, and the sage was he
who is now Devadatta. Thanks to that teacher, my friend
Devadatta, I was able to complete my practices and attain the
enlightenment to save others. Therefore in the future, after a
long time has passed, Devadatta will become a Buddha
named Heavenly-King (Devaraja). He will explain the Wonderful Law to countless numbers of living beings and lead
them to awakening. That Buddha (Devadatta) will influence
the world even after he has entered nirvana. People will come
from afar to his stupa, and there they will be spiritually awakened. . . .

If there are good men and women in the future, who hear
this Chapter of Devadatta, and respect it faithfully without any

doubt in their minds, they will not fall into the realms of hell or the states of hungry spirits or animals; instead, they will be reborn before the Buddhas of the ten directions. At the places of their rebirth, this Sutra will always be heard. If they are born in the heavens, they will enjoy wonderful pleasures. If they are born before a Buddha, they will appear spontaneously from a lotus flower (p. 195-198).

This story seems to tell us that the good and evil in people is not fixed and absolute, but is developed by human relationships and the times in which people live. Devadatta was not entirely evil. Accounts tell us that he was strict—too strict, perhaps—in his self-discipline. (Perhaps he became a traitor because of his personal shortcomings. He might also have been influenced by other people in the Sangha who held personal grudges against the Buddha.) Recent historical studies reveal that other religious groups were then being organized in that same part of India. (The strictly ascetic Jains, for instance, whose followers still exist, were already widely known. Sakyamuni, who taught a middle way between the extremes of severe asceticism on the one hand and license on the other, sometimes met their leaders and debated with them. Was Devadatta influenced by them or others like them?)

Political scandals have always been with us. But the politicians, themselves, rarely think of themselves as scandalous. They are only "back scratching," they feel: repaying a favor for a favor. The country may not forgive them for putting selfish interests ahead of national interests, but we cannot say that they were entirely evil for helping their political friends. They put human relationships ahead of duty.

The relationship between Sakyamuni and Devadatta can be considered an example of human relationships. Devadatta was a traitor during Sakyamuni's lifetime. However, in a previous life he had been an indispensable teacher of Sakyamuni. Buddhism believes that good and evil are not two separate things; there is no absolute distinction between the two. An evil deed cannot be considered an absolute. The Devadatta Chapter is known as the teaching that explains the attainment of enlightenment by evil people, and its philosophical background comes from the "non-duality of good and evil," as understood in Buddhism.

After Sakyamuni preached the story of Devadatta, Accumulated-Wisdom Bodhisattva (Prajnakuta) who was accompanying Many-Treasures Buddha approached that Buddha and asked if it was time for them to return to their own world. Hearing this, Sakyamuni said to Accumulated-Wisdom, "Wait! Speak first with Manjusri Bodhisattva about the Wonderful Law, and then you may return home."

Manjusri, sitting on a thousand-petaled lotus flower as large as a wheel, then emerged from the palace of a dragon-king beneath the sea, and rose into the sky. Reaching Mount Sacred Eagle, he descended from the lotus flower to venerate the two Buddhas, Sakyamuni and Many-Treasures, who were seated in the Stupa of Treasures. After paying his respects, he went down to Accumulated-Wisdom, exchanged greetings with him, and sat down beside him (p. 198-9).

Accumulated-Wisdom asked him, "I see that you have come from the palace of a dragon-king beneath the sea. How many beings did you teach there?" Manjusri answered, "The number is so great that I can neither express it in words nor calculate it. But if you wait for a moment, I will show you."

No sooner had he finished speaking, when numerous Bodhisattvas, seated on lotus flowers, emerged from the sea. They traveled to Mount Sacred Eagle, and remained in the sky. All of them had been taught by Manjusri beneath the sea.

Accumulated-Wisdom was so impressed that he praised Manjusri in verses: "O Possessor of great wisdom and virtue! I see now that you have led and inspired countless living beings. You preach the true teachings, explain the Dharma of the One Vehicle, and lead many beings to attain enlightenment."

"I taught only the Lotus Sutra," replied Manjusri. "Yes," said Accumulated-Wisdom, "it is indeed a rare and profound teaching. But can people attain enlightenment quickly by the teachings of this Sutra?"

Manjusri answered, "Yes, indeed! The daughter of Sagara the Dragon-King did just that. She is only eight years old, but she is wise; her faculties are sharp; and she understands the needs of other beings. She accepted all the teachings of the Buddha and mastered the truth. She aspired for instantaneous enlightenment (Bodhi) and reached the stage of irrevocability, from which she can never slip back. She preaches the Dharma eloquently and loves people as if they were her own children. She is compassionate, humble, gentle, graceful, and already qualified to attain Bodhi."

Accumulated-Wisdom was skeptical. "Looking at everything that Sakyamuni Buddha has experienced," he said, "I can see that he spent a very long time practicing austerities. He accumulated virtue, sought Bodhi without rest, did not spare even his life to serve living beings, and then finally became a Buddha. I can hardly believe that the daughter of a dragon-king can attain enlightenment in such a short time!"

Hardly had he finished speaking, when the Dragon-King's daughter appeared in front of Sakyamuni. She bowed before him, and chanted verses in his praise (p. 200-201).

Then Sariputra (the wisest of the Buddha's sravaka-disciples) said to her,

> You say that you will soon attain Buddhahood, but I can hardly believe that. Everybody knows that women are unable to understand the Dharma and be awakened. Also, in order to attain enlightenment, an infinitely long period of practice is required. Besides, it is well known that women by nature have five impossibilities; they cannot enter five superior existences: a Brahman heavenly-king, a King Sakra, a King Mara, a "wheel-turning" (powerful) holy king, or a Buddha (all of whom are males). How could you possibly attain enlightenment?

The Dragon-King's daughter possessed a gem as valuable as the whole world. She offered it to the Buddha, and immediately he accepted it. The young girl then turned to Accumulated-Wisdom and Sariputra, saying to them, "Watch me and see for yourselves! I can attain enlightenment much quicker that the World-Honored One accepted my gem." In no time, she transformed herself into a boy, went to the south where it was not polluted, sat down on a jeweled lotus, and attained enlightenment. She acquired the thirty-two physical marks of a Buddha, and expounded the Dharma to living beings.

Seeing this, people bowed joyfully before her. Many of them reached the stage of irrevocability, and were guaranteed their future attainment of enlightenment. All the others who were present, including Accumulated-Wisdom and Sariputra, accepted what they saw and believed in silence (p. 201-2).

The story of how the Dragon-King's daughter attained enlightenment has long been taken as an example of women attaining enlightenment by instantly understanding the Dharma. In India, it was thought that women were spiritually inferior to men, and could not enter any of the five superior existences—Buddhahood being one of them. However, Sakyamuni taught that all living beings—male or female, young or old, human or nonhuman—are potential Buddhas. This story graphically illustrates his point, and it helped future generations overcome their prejudice against women.

The Buddha is a perfected being with a human personality. He is the ideal toward which all human beings strive. It had long been believed that to become such a perfect being takes an endlessly long period of training and practice. But the daughter of the Dragon-King attained enlightenment quickly. Her case is called, "The Attainment of Buddhahood in This Very Life." It maintains that ordinary people have the possibility to attain enlightenment in their own bodies (during their present lifetimes), and teaches that the Buddha's power works within the bodies of ordinary people. The idea of "the attainment of Buddhahood in this life" greatly influenced Japanese society after the Great Master Dengyo introduced it from China in 805. Dengyo, a Japanese scholar, had already read about it in the Lotus Sutra, but he found that the Chinese had worked it out in detail. Also, Nichiren explained this idea in *Kanjin-honzon-sho* ("A Treatise Revealing the Spiritual Contemplation of the Most-Venerable-One"). In it he says, "Sakyamuni Buddha, who has attained Perfect Enlightenment, is our flesh and blood, and all the merits he has accumulated before and after attaining Buddhahood are our bones."

However, it would be a serious mistake to take the teaching of the "attainment of Buddhahood in this life" as meaning we can attain enlightenment without any effort. Even if we believe strongly in a religion, we must still practice it and apply its principles to our life. But by the power of their faith, ordinary people can attain the power of the Buddha without first completing difficult studies and practicing for eons and eons. This is what is meant by the "attainment of Buddhahood in this very life."

The Sutra of the Lotus Flower of the Wonderful Law

CHAPTER XIII: ENCOURAGEMENT FOR KEEPING THIS SUTRA

(The Assembly in the Sky)

"Encouragement for Keeping This Sutra" means encouraging people to uphold it in spite of certain difficulties. It also implies effort and patience. In Chapter Eleven, "Beholding the Stupa of Treasures," Sakyamuni called out to the crowd from the Stupa of Treasures, "Is there anyone here who is willing to expound the Lotus Sutra in this Saha-world ("World of Endurance") after my death, and overcome all difficulties? If there is, I will transmit the Sutra to that person." Responding to his words, many bodhisattvas promised to spread the Sutra in the evil world after the Buddha's extinction, and they spoke about their resolution. This is the theme of this chapter.

Chapter Thirteen should really follow Chapter Eleven, but Chapter Twelve, "Devadatta," has been inserted between them. Chapter Eleven emphasizes the difficulty of spreading the Sutra after Sakyamuni's extinction, and Chapter Thirteen reiterates this theme and shows the great power of the Sutra.

Thereupon Medicine-King Bodhisattva and Great-Eloquence Bodhisattva, together with their twenty thousand attendants who were also bodhisattvas, appeared before the Buddha and said to him, "Please do not worry! We will expound this Sutra. In the evil world after your extinction, living beings may have unclear minds and roots of evil, so teaching them will not be easy. But we will be patient and not spare any efforts to expound the Sutra."

There were also present five hundred arhats and eight thousand "hearers," some having more to learn and others having nothing more to learn. Both the arhats and the "hearers" had already been assured of their future attainment of enlightenment, and they volunteered to expound the Sutra in other worlds beyond this one.

Among this congregation were Sakyamuni's step-mother, Great Prajapati, and his former wife, Yasodhara, with their attending nuns. They, too, were eager to receive assurance of their future buddhahood. Sakyamuni read their minds and gave them the assurance they desired. Thereupon the nuns, too, offered to expound the Sutra in other worlds (p. 203-4).

At this time, there were eighty billion nayuta of bodhisattvas who had already reached a high level of accomplishment, called the stage of irrevocability. They also made up their minds to expound the Sutra by following the directions of the World-Honored One. They approached the Buddha and together steadfastly recited an oath in verses (p. 205).

World-Honored One, please do not worry! We will expound this Sutra in the evil world after your extinction. There will be difficulties, we know.

(1) All kinds of ignorant people will speak ill of us, the expounders of the Sutra. They may even attack us with swords and clubs, but we will endure it.

(2) There will be cunning monks who think that they have obtained what they have not. Their minds will be filled with arrogance, and they will abuse us.

(3) Some monks will live in remote, quiet places, pretending to practice the Way, but really despising ordinary people. They will be greedy for money, and expound the Dharma for pay. People will respect them like arhats who have attained supernatural powers. These spiritual leaders will criticize us and tell everybody, "Those monks are expounding the Sutra only to get wealth and fame. They deceive people and make up their own sutra (claiming to have received it from the

Buddha), because they hope to make a profit from it." They will encourage powerful people, such as kings, ministers, and Brahmans, to persecute us.

We know that difficulties such as these will happen. But we will endure everything because we respect the Buddha. We will also ignore their spiteful words. In this evil world, all sorts of dreadful things can happen (to make people behave like this). For example, devils can enter their minds, causing them to curse and insult us. But we will wear the armor of endurance because we respect and believe in the Buddha. All of us are ready to say, "We don't care about our bodies or our lives. All we treasure is unsurpassed enlightenment."

In the later days (the Age of Degeneration), there might be evil monks who cannot understand the teachings that the Buddha has expounded expediently. They may drive us out of our temples and monasteries. However, we will ignore such difficulties and concentrate on our mission.

Because we are the messengers of the World-Honored One, we are fearless of any danger. We solemnly vow that we will expound the Dharma at any cost (p. 206-9).

Thus the eighty billion nayuta of never-faltering bodhisattvas told their decision to Sakyamuni. The first three types of persecutors listed above are examples of "arrogance of people who are sure of their own virtue." The first group consists of ordinary people, the second of clergy, and the third of hermits, ascetics who have renounced the world, and leaders among the clergy. These three groups are the three types of people who will persecute expounders of the Dharma during the Age of Degeneration. From olden times, they have been called the "three kinds of powerful enemies." "Arrogance of people who are sure of their own virtue" is seen in people who are proud of their own positions and hostile toward the Teaching of Equality revealed in the Lotus Sutra. Through the words of these eighty billion nayuta of bodhisattvas, Sakyamuni foretold that such evil people, consisting of both clergy and laity, will appear in the world after his extinction, be hostile to the Lotus Sutra, and vigorously oppose anyone who attempts to propagate it.

The Lotus Sutra has teachings that prophesy the future after the Buddha's extinction. These teachings are unique to this Sutra, and are not found in other sutras to such an extent. The prophecy tells us that the world after the extinction of the Buddha will be an evil place—an Age of Degeneration—in which expounders of the Lotus Sutra can expect to suffer troubles and even persecution. That they must overcome these troubles and expound the Lotus Sutra to make this Saha-world into the Pure Land of the Buddha, is not just a prophecy. It is a major teaching. The preceding verses recited by the never-faltering bodhisattvas represent this teaching. It is called the "Twenty Verses of Chapter Thirteen."

The Age of Degeneration lies in the future after Sakyamuni's earthly lifetime. It does not denote a specific era. Whenever we ordinary people reflect seriously on the quality of our lives, we realize that we live far from the spirit of the Buddha. Our minds are soiled with evil and illusions. This actual state of human beings is what is called the Age of Degeneration. The Lotus Sutra warns us that it will be our normal state once the Buddha has departed from among us.

Sakyamuni told us in the Lotus Sutra how we should live. We "read" the Sutra by comparing its teachings with our deeds. It was Nichiren (1220-1280) who completed the practice of "reading" the Lotus Sutra and fulfilling it in deeds throughout his lifetime. As you may know, Nichiren endured many persecutions, but he understood his troubles as having been foretold in the Lotus Sutra. Experiencing them, he realized that Sakyamuni's prophecies had proven to be true. Instead of lamenting his fate, he derived spiritual joy at being allowed to fulfill the prophecies in his own body.

On September 12, 1271, the military government at Kamakura arrested Nichiren arbitrarily and took him to the place of execution, called Tatsu-no-kuchi ("the dragon's mouth"). When one of his assailants found scrolls of the Lotus Sutra in Nichiren's pocket, he hit Nichiren on the face with one of them. Nichiren realized that this scroll was the one containing the same chapter we have just been reading, "Encouragement for Keeping the Sutra." At first he felt humiliated at being struck in the face, but when he realized which scroll it was, he rejoiced instead. By coincidence, he was being beaten by the same scroll which predicted such a fate for one who propagates the Sutra.

The twenty verses in Chapter Thirteen had much influence on Nichiren. He mentions them in his treatise, Kaimoku-sho ("Opening the Eyes"). "If I had not been born in this country," he says, "the twenty verses in Chapter Thirteen would not have been proven, the World-Honored One would have seemed to be a great liar, and the eighty billion nayuta of bodhisattvas would have fallen into the sin of lying, too. Just as the Lotus Sutra foretold, I was often driven out (into exile). The word 'often' in the Sutra came true. This word was not experienced by either Tendai (Great Master Chih-i of China) or Dengyo (Great Master Saicho of Japan), not to speak of lesser people. I, Nichiren, alone read them from experience. For I perfectly fit the Buddha's description of the person spreading the Lotus Sutra 'in the dreadful and evil world' at the beginning of the Latter Age."

That is to say, Nichiren was the only person who read, experienced, and dedicated his life to the real meanings of the verses of Chapter Thirteen.

The Sutra of the Lotus Flower of the Wonderful Law

CHAPTER XIV: PEACEFUL PRACTICES

(The Assembly in the Sky)

"Peaceful practices" designates ways to preach and spread the Sutra while keeping your body and mind relaxed and peaceful. The chapter discusses four kinds of peaceful practices: those of body, mouth, mind, and resolution (vows).

The previous chapter has explained that anyone who preaches and spreads the Lotus Sutra in the future, the Age of Degeneration, must have stamina. Such a person must resolve to spread the Sutra even though evil people, known as the Three Strong Enemies, will appear in his or her path to trouble or even persecute him. This way of propagation, by confronting the Three Strong Enemies head-on, may strain the preacher's relationships with others. By way of contrast, there is another practical way to spread the Dharma, with an attitude that is calmer and more relaxed. This attitude is called, "Peaceful Practices."

Manjusri Bodhisattva asked the Buddha, "These extraordinary Bodhisattvas have made a great resolution to expound this Lotus Sutra in the evil world because they are following you respectfully. How should an ordinary Bodhi-sattva expound this Sutra in the evil world?"

The Buddha answered by saying, "A Bodhisattva should practice four sets of things (p. 210)."

These four are:

(1) *Peaceful Practices of the Body.* This means acting always with restraint. The Buddha divides these peaceful

115

practices into two parts: "performing proper practices" and
"approaching proper things."

The first means doing good deeds. Bodhisattvas should
always practice the virtue of patience, be mild and gentle,
and see things as they truly are.

The second, "approach proper things," indicates how a
Bodhisattva should relate to people—that is, his sphere of
associations. The Sutra delineates ten points:

1. The Bodhisattva should avoid persons with great political
power, such as kings, ministers, or other high government
officials.
2. He should not approach those who preach heresy, or who
waste time writing about worldly affairs.
3. He should not approach people who entertain the public
by risking their lives or the lives of others.
4. He should not approach those who make their living by
killing living beings.
5. He should not approach, question, or stay with any persons
who seek the teaching of the Lesser Vehicle. If he is approached by them, he should expound the Dharma with mod-
eration, but not request any payment.
6. He should not expound the Dharma to any woman he desires.
7. He should not approach eunuchs.
8. He should never enter anyone's house uninvited.
9. He should not be too friendly with a woman, even to expound the Dharma to her.
10. He should not keep young children with him.

The Bodhisattva should always be willing to teach such
people if they ask him, but he should not seek them out or
ask for any payment from them. He or she should take pleasure in meditation and, in a quiet place, practice to control
the mind (p. 211).

This is the first way to approach proper things. The Buddha also teaches a second way to approach proper things: the

Bodhisattva should understand that all things are insubstantial, inexplicable, formless, not born, and without property. "Things can exist only by dependent origination" (p. 212).

(2) *Peaceful Practices of the Mouth* are to choose words carefully and make no mistakes in expounding the Dharma. There are four points:

1. A Bodhisattva should not point out the faults of other sutras or their adherents.
2. He or she should not despise other preachers of the Dharma.
3. He or she should not speak of either the merits or the demerits of other preachers, and should not mention "hearers" by name when criticizing their teachings or even when praising them.
4. He or she should not feel hostile toward anybody, and should freely answer any questions put to him. When asked difficult questions, the Bodhisattva should not answer by the teachings of the Lesser Vehicle, but always refer to the Great Vehicle, and so lead people to the "knowledge of the equality and differences of all things" (p. 216).

(3) *Peaceful Practices of the Mind* mean maintaining the right mental attitude while expounding the Dharma. There are four points.

1. A Bodhisattva must not be jealous of others, or flatter them, or deceive them.
2. He or she should not despise anyone who studies the Way to Buddhahood by any other method, speak ill of them, or point out their faults.
3. He or she should not disturb or perplex those who seek any of the Three Vehicles ("hearers," self-enlightened Buddhas, or practicers of the Way of the Bodhisattvas), and never tell them, "You are far from enlightenment. You cannot attain the knowledge of the equality and differences of all things

because you are licentious and lazy in seeking enlightenment."
4. A Bodhisattva should not get involved in meaningless quar-
rels with the followers of other schools of thought (p. 218).

Instead of getting bogged down in stupid arguments, a
Bodhisattva should have great compassion toward all living
beings. He should look upon all the Buddhas as his loving
parents, and upon all the Bodhisattvas as his great teachers.
He or she should expound the Dharma to all living beings
without showing any partiality (p. 218-219).

(4) *Peaceful Practices of Resolution* is to resolve solemnly to make every effort to realize and spread the Lotus
Sutra in the Age of Degeneration, or the evil world of the
future. There are three points.

1. The Bodhisattva should have great loving-kindness toward
both clergy and laity, and great compassion toward those
who are not Bodhisattvas. (This is called the subject of resolution.)
2. The reason is that people do not understand that the Buddha expounded expedient teachings according to the capacities of living beings, and they neither believe it nor understand it. (This is the reason for resolution.)
3. Therefore, when a Bodhisattva attains supreme-perfect-enlightenment, he or she will resolve to lead all people to the
Lotus Sutra, and by means of his acquired supernatural powers and wisdom, cause them to understand the law (p. 220).

After Sakyamuni expounded the four sets of peaceful
practices, he said that those who carried out these four sets in
the Age of Degeneration, or the evil world in the future,
would be praised by all kinds of people. They will be accompanied and protected by heavenly beings, who will gather to
hear the Dharma from them. Then Sakyamuni taught that the
Lotus Sutra is the supreme teaching, superior to any

others. He did this by means of another parable, this one called "A Brilliant Gem in the Top-knot."

Suppose a powerful wheel-turning-holy-king, a king superlative in war and peace, threatened neighboring monarchies and demanded their surrender. They ignored his demands, so he led his troops against them and defeated them by force of arms. He was pleased to see that some of his officers and men distinguished themselves in the war. Therefore, he rewarded each of them according to what they had earned, granting them spoils of war and other gifts, such as lands, villages, castles, palaces, and treasures. But there was one thing which he did not give away to anyone. This was a brilliant gem which he wore in his top-knot—a gem unique in all the world. If he had given it away, his followers would have been shocked (for it symbolized the authority of the king himself).

The Buddha is like that king. He obtained the world of the Dharma (true law) by his powers of dhyana-concentration and wisdom, and became king of the "triple world" (of desires, form, and non-form). He demanded that the evil spirits surrender and cease harassing living beings, but they ignored his demands. Therefore he waged war against them, and his armies, led by his outstanding disciples, launched themselves into battle with the forces of evil. He was pleased to see that some of his disciples distinguished themselves in the combat. He expounded many sutras for them, gave them treasures from the Dharma, and led them to Nirvana. But he did not expound the Lotus Sutra to them. Only when he sees that his disciples have already obtained extraordinary merits in their fight with the evil ones, and that they have already eliminated cravings and illusion, left the "triple world," and destroyed the nets of the demons (maras), does he then joyfully expound this Lotus Sutra, leading them to perfect enlightenment.

The Lotus Sutra is the treasury of the hidden core of the Buddhas. It is superior to all other sutras. I kept it in secret and refrained from expounding it throughout the long night. Now

for the first time I remove it from my top-knot and give it to
you all (p. 221-2).

After these words, Sakyamuni concludes by stating the
rewards which will accrue to those who uphold the Sutra in
the future:

> Anyone who reads this Sutra will be free from grief, sor-
> row, disease, or pain. His complexion will be fair. He will be
> neither poor, humble, nor ugly. Living beings will want to see
> him just as they want to see sages and saints. Celestial pages
> will serve him. He will not be struck with swords or sticks. He
> will not be poisoned. If anyone speaks ill of him, that
> speaker's mouth will be shut. The reader of this Sutra will be
> able to travel far and wide as fearlessly as a lion king. The
> light of his wisdom will be as bright as sunlight (p. 224).

Thus the Sutra says that anyone who reads, recites, and
expounds the Lotus Sutra will be attractive in appearance,
fearless, safe from accidents, and served by angels from
heaven. It goes on to say that the figure of the Buddha will
appear in the dreams of such a person, lead him or her to
renounce the world, attain enlightenment, and enter Nirvana
just as the Buddha does.

This is an outline of the chapter called "Peaceful Practices." The message of this chapter stands in contrast with that
of the previous chapter, "Encouragement for Keeping the
Sutra." In that chapter, we recall, the Sutra tells us that we
should be ready to accept any difficulty, and endure patiently
if we come under persecution while spreading the Sutra. This
also means that, in order to spread the Sutra, we must try to
convince and convert someone who may be causing us problems. Later, in Chapter Twenty, "Never-Despise Bodhisattva,"
the Sutra will tell us about a Bodhisattva named Never-Despise, who used to bow to and respect everyone he met,
preaching the law to them, even when they hit him or threw
stones at him. Great Master Chih-i and Nichiren called such

ways of spreading the Dharma, *shakubuku*, meaning "converting others by persistent preaching." On the other hand, spreading the law by peaceful practices, as described in this chapter, is called *shoju*, "accepting." *Shakubuku* is the way to reproach opponents for their errors and make them awaken from their illusions. *Shoju* is to lead and convince them by respectfully accepting and understanding their viewpoints and situations. The difference between these two ways of propagation depends on the times and the abilities of the hearers to understand. Although the two methods seem to be entirely different, they have the same aim—to save others. Therefore, they share the same spirit.

In the history of Buddhism, Great Master Chih-i generally undertook the way of *shoju*, and Nichiren generally practiced the way of *shakubuku*. However, Chih-i also valued the spirit of *shakubuku*, and Nichiren also gave importance to the spirit of *shoju*. In our times, the way of *shoju* seems more appropriate, but it must be flavored with the spirit of *shakubuku*, too.

The Sutra of the Lotus Flower of the Wonderful Law

CHAPTER XV: THE APPEARANCE OF BODHISATTVAS FROM UNDERGROUND

(The Assembly in the Sky)

The name of this chapter actually means that Bodhisattvas "spring up from underground." The scene of the chapter depicts countless Bodhisattvas welling up like clouds around Sakyamuni.

We recall that in Chapter Eleven, "Beholding the Stupa of Treasures," Sakyamuni had appealed from within the stupa to the congregation. "Is there anyone here," he asked, "who is willing to expound the Lotus Sutra in the world after my extinction? I wish to hand it on to someone so that it can be perpetuated." In Chapter Thirteen, "Encouragement for Keeping the Sutra," eighty thousand Bodhisattvas of superior quality, such as Medicine-King Bodhisattva, and eighty thousand billion other great Bodhisattvas respond to his appeal and offer to keep and spread the Sutra in our world. But Sakyamuni did not answer them. Instead, he went on to expound Chapter Fourteen, "Peaceful Practices." As Chapter Fifteen begins, countless Bodhisattvas, "more than eight times the number of sands in the River Ganges," stand up before the Buddha and reiterate their offer to spread the Sutra. "We are the ones," they promise, "who will disseminate the Lotus Sutra in this World of Endurance." But Sakyamuni gives them an unexpected answer:

"No," he said, "You don't need to protect or uphold this Sutra, because there are (already) Bodhisattvas in this World

123

of Endurance, as many as sixty thousand times the number of sands in the River Ganges, and they are the ones who will assume the responsibility for disseminating the Sutra in this Saha-world."

No sooner had he spoken these words, when the ground quaked and cracked, and countless Bodhisattvas emerged from beneath the earth like clouds, and sprang up into the air. All of these extraordinary beings were golden colored. They emitted brilliant rays of light, and displayed the "thirty-two marks of Buddhas."

These Bodhisattvas had existed in the void beneath the World of Endurance. They had emerged because they heard the voice of Sakyamuni. Each of them was the leader of a great multitude, and was accompanied by as many attendants as sixty times the number of sands in the River Ganges.

Each of the Bodhisattvas who had sprung up soared into the sky, approached Many-Treasures Buddha and Sakyamuni in the Stupa of Treasures, and bowed before them. They also venerated each of the manifestations of Sakyamuni Buddha, who had come from the ten directions in space, and praised them all as only Bodhisattvas know how to praise Buddhas. During this time, Sakyamuni and all the assembly remained silent. A long time passed—about fifty small kalpas—but the supernatural powers of Sakyamuni made the congregation feel as if it were only half a day.

Among these great Bodhisattvas filling the sky, there were four who were the leaders. Their names were Superb-Action, Limitless-Action, Pure-Action, and Steadily-Established-Action. They pressed their hands together in adoration, looked up at Sakyamuni, and greeted him. "World-Honored One! Are you in good health? Are you at ease? Do those whom you educated accept the teachings easily, or do they fail to comprehend and give you cause for worry?" The World-Honored One replied, "No, they are all right. They follow my teachings obediently" (p. 228-230).

Observing all this, the other Bodhisattvas were bewildered. "Countless Bodhisattvas have sprung up from underground," they murmured to each other. "Who are they? We have never seen any of them before. This is, indeed, strange!" Then Maitreya Bodhisattva, representing the others, asked Sakyamuni, "Who are all these Bodhisattvas? They are the most marvelous Bodhisattvas any of us have ever seen. Where did they come from, and why did they come here? Please explain it to us!"

Other Bodhisattvas in the congregation, those who had come from the ten directions of space accompanying the duplicate Buddhas, were just as puzzled. They put the same question to their respective Buddhas. Their Buddhas told them, "Sakyamuni Buddha will answer Maitreya Bodhisattva. Listen to him attentively" (p. 231-34).

The answer given by Sakyamuni reveals a singular teaching. He prefaces his explanation by saying, "Maitreya, you have asked a vital question. Pay close attention and accept by faith what I am about to say." Then he explains:

"It is true that you have never seen any of these countless Bodhisattvas who have sprung up from beneath the earth. But I, Sakyamuni, have been teaching them in the World of Endurance ever since I attained Buddhahood. They are my spiritual children. They reject the clamor of crowds and wish to be in quiet places, chant the sutras, and constantly practice my teachings. They are resolute in fulfilling their vows (to save all beings), purifying themselves, and always seeking supreme wisdom. It may appear to you as if, after I attained Buddhahood under the Bodhi tree near the city of Gaya, I then taught them for the first time, and let them enter the Way to Buddhahood. But to tell the truth, I have been expounding the law to them since time immemorial" (p. 235-37).

This answer elicits a new question from Maitreya Bodhisattva and the others. "Only forty years have passed since the World-Honored One renounced his princely throne, set forth on the path to enlightenment, and was awakened at the place of enlightenment near the city of Gaya. During such a short period of time, it is impossible to have led such a tremendous number of Bodhisattvas as we

have seen here springing up from under the earth. Such a
thing is unbelievable.

"For example, suppose a young man of twenty-five, handsome and with jet black hair, were to point to an old centenar-
ian and say, 'This is my son.' Or suppose the one hundred
year old man were to point to that young man and say, 'This is
my father, the one who enlightened me.' Either case would be
ridiculous, and we would not believe it" (p. 237-8).

In the chapter which follows, Sakyamuni will answer
this logical objection. He will explain the important concept
of the Original Buddha who attained Buddhahood in the remotest past. The Buddha, who is eternal, attained Nirvana
ages ago, and since then he has led people in the World of
Endurance.

Maitreya Bodhisattva repeats his questions in verses.
Among his verses, which describe the Bodhisattvas who have
sprung up from beneath the earth, the following are often
quoted:

These sons of yours are countless. They have practiced the
Way to Buddhahood for ages. They have attained wisdom
and supernatural powers. They have perfected the Way of
Bodhisattvas. They are no more defiled by worldly desires
than a lotus blossom is by the water in which it grows. They
sprang up from beneath the earth and now stand respectfully
before you (p. 238-9).

Ascetics of Hinayana Buddhism (the Lesser Vehicle) aim
to escape from our world of sorrows, stand aloof from its
problems, and attain a pure state of consciousness. This can
make them indifferent to the world. They easily forget to fulfill the most important task in religion, namely, to save ordinary people.

On the other hand, Mahayana Buddhism (the Great Vehicle), beginning from the point of view of ordinary people,
asserts that the state of enlightenment can be realized only in

the midst of this world, because Bodhisattvas cannot save people without living and working here where evil and misery exist. Bodhisattvas, of course, are themselves pure, and they are never contaminated by the vice and evil of their environments. They are like lovely lotus flowers, which rise from out of the mud at the bottom of the water.

It is said that the dirtier the pond from which it grows, the more beautifully a lotus blooms. The flower is itself pure and unaffected by the mud from which it has sprung. The Sutra tells us that the method of Bodhisattva-practice should be similar to that of a lotus flower. It can be said that "lotus flower," which is part of the title (Daimoku) of the Lotus Sutra ("The Sutra of the Lotus Flower of the Wonderful Law"), symbolizes this ideal Bodhisattva-practice.

This is a summary of the chapter, "The Appearance of Bodhisattvas from Underground." It is important to note that the Bodhisattvas who sprang up from beneath the earth, who first appear in this chapter, are not recognized by anyone in the congregation, not even by Maitreya, who is destined to be our next Buddha. These great Bodhisattvas appear only in this sutra and not in any other. Only these Bodhisattvas, who sprang up from beneath the earth, have the qualifications necessary to spread the Lotus Sutra in the evil and degenerate World of Endurance. Later on, in Chapter Twenty-one, "Supernatural Powers of the Tathagata," Sakyamuni will transmit the Lotus Sutra directly to them.

Here it is revealed that the Bodhisattvas who sprang up from beneath the earth are the exemplary Bodhisattvas of the Lotus Sutra. Many other Bodhisattvas have appeared before this chapter, but these are the only ones who fully live up to the Sutra's teachings. Thus they symbolize the ideal, the models for dynamic activity. Their sphere of action is summarized in the lines, "They are no more defiled by worldly desires than a lotus flower is by the water in which it grows."

According to *Kamon*, which is an ancient method of analyzing the Lotus Sutra, the first half of the Sutra, consisting of fourteen chapters, is called *Shakumon*—teachings "derived" from a source (*shaku* literally means "footprint;" *mon* is "gate"). The second half, consisting of the final fourteen chapters, is known as *Honmon* or *Hommon*—the "Primary Gate" or Primary Mystery (*hon* means "root" or "source"). This second half reveals the Original and Eternal Buddha (*Kuon Hombutsu*). The appearance of the Bodhisattvas from Underground (*Jiyu-no-bosatsu*, literally "Bodhisattvas who well up from the earth") is an introduction to the second half of the Sutra; and the next chapter, "The Duration of the Life of the Tathagata," is its principal part.

That is to say, this chapter presents the ideal Bodhisattvas in the persons of the Bodhisattvas from Underground. The following chapter, the "Duration of the Life of the Tathagata," reveals the true nature of the Buddha (the Original and Eternal Buddha) and his true Pure Land. It is none other than this Saha-world of ours. Thus the "Duration of the Life of the Tathagata" will emerge as the Sutra's heart and center.

The Sutra of the Lotus Flower of the Wonderful Law

CHAPTER XVI: THE DURATION OF THE LIFE OF THE TATHAGATA

(The Assembly in the Sky)

"The Duration of the Life of the Tathagata" (pronounced Tut-HAH-gut-tuh), is the name of this chapter, which teaches that the Buddha is eternal. We ordinary people usually think that the Buddha had a limited existence, just as we have. It is commonly understood that Sakyamuni was born a prince in the kingdom of the Sakya clan in the Himalayan foothills about 2,500 years ago. When he was around thirty years old, he renounced the world, attained enlightenment after six years of training, and became the Buddha at the place of enlightenment, now known as Buddha-gaya. Afterwards, he expounded the Dharma throughout northern India, and entered Nirvana at the age of eighty. But this limited Sakyamuni, who is equivalent to Sakyamuni as a historical personage, is a provisional figure. This chapter of the "Duration of the Life of the Tathagata (the "One Thus Come"), reveals that he is an everlasting and immortal being, possessing eternal life. This assertion has always been considered the pivotal teaching of the Lotus Sutra.

In the previous chapter, countless Bodhisattvas sprang up from underground. This chapter tells why they appeared. It is presented as an answer to the questions posed by Maitreya Bodhisattva, when he wondered about the marvelous phenomenon which he and his companions had witnessed. It asserts that the Buddha's lifetime is eternal.

129

Sakyamuni begins the chapter by appealing three times for his listeners to "understand my sincere and infallible words by faith." To this appeal, all the Bodhisattvas headed by Maitreya responded each time, "World-Honored One, tell us! We will receive your words by faith." Then Sakyamuni replied, "Listen to me attentively! I will reveal to you my hidden core and supernatural powers" (p. 241).

Here "hidden core" means his deepest innermost self, and "supernatural powers" are actions outflowing from that hidden core.

> Everybody in the world, even the deities in heaven and demons (*asuras*), think that Sakyamuni was born at the palace of the Sakya kingdom, renounced the world, sat at the place of meditation near the city of Gaya, attained supreme enlightenment, and became the Buddha. However, in reality it has been an infinite time, comparable to one hundred thousand millions of billions of asamkhyas of eons, since I (Sakyamuni) became the Buddha.
>
> For instance, suppose someone were to collect five hundred thousand million billion Sumeru-worlds (universes, each containing a billion worlds), smash them, and grind them into dust. Then he picked up each particle of dust and put it at a place five hundred thousand million billions of eons to the east. He put another particle of the dust at a place another five hundred thousand million billion eons further east, and repeated the process until all the particles were exhausted. In this case, how many worlds would he pass? Do you think their number could be calculated, or not?

Maitreya Bodhisattva replied,

> We cannot count or even imagine such a huge number. It is far beyond the wisdom of all the Sravakas and Pratyeka Buddhas or Bodhisattvas such as ourselves. Even those of us who have reached the stage of never again slipping back, could never conceive such a number.

Accepting this reply, Sakyamuni went to increase the numbers even more.

> Good men! Now I will tell you clearly. Suppose these worlds, whether they were marked with particles of dust or not, were smashed into dust. The number of the kalpas which have elapsed since I became the Buddha is one hundred thousand billion nayuta asamkhyas larger than the number of particles of the dust thus produced. All this time, I have been living in the World of Endurance, teaching [the living beings of this world] by expounding the Dharma to them. I also have been leading and benefiting the living beings of one hundred thousand billion nayuta asamkhya worlds outside this world (p. 242).

By means of these enormous numbers, numbers far beyond the ability of mathematics to conceive, Sakyamuni compares his life span to eternity. The simile which he uses is commonly called the "Five Hundred Dust-atom Kalpas."

We usually think that Sakyamuni led a limited existence, was born in India over two millennia ago, and died there at the age of eighty. This is correct as far as history goes. But from the essential standpoint, such a limited existence is not the true form of Sakyamuni. An eternal and immortal existence, which exists within and beyond the limited one, is the substance of Sakyamuni Buddha. The vital point of this chapter, "The Duration of the Life of the Tathagata," is that Sakyamuni, as a historical figure, declares that his essence is eternal and immeasurable. This declaration, the salient feature of the Lotus Sutra, cannot be found in any other sutra.

Sakyamuni continues his explanation:

> During all this time, I gave myself various names, for instance, Burning-Light Buddha (Dipankara, who is said to have been the last Buddha to appear in our world before Sakyamuni). I also announced, "That Buddha has entered into Nirvana." I did all these things only as expedients.

> When people came to me, I could discern with my Bud-
> dha-eyes the strength of their faith and other faculties. To help
> them, I called myself by different names, told them differently
> about the duration of my life, and said that I would enter
> Nirvana (disappear from their world) in ways which they
> could understand. I also expounded the Wonderful Law with
> these expedients, and caused living beings to rejoice (p. 242).

In Buddhism, people worship not only Sakyamuni Buddha but also other Buddhas, such as Amitayus (in the west)
and Aksobhya (in the east). Such Buddhas have different
names and attributes, and different life spans, long or short.
The longest existing one is thought to have lived for several
tens of kalpas. At any rate, they are all limited entities, because all of them eventually entered into Nirvana. The main
point of the Lotus Sutra is that all Buddhas, by whatever
names they may use, are temporary manifestations of the
eternal, infinite, and immortal Sakyamuni Buddha. He transforms himself into other Buddhas when necessary to redeem
and guide people, who understand him in various ways according to their particular times, places, and levels of culture.

This eternal and immortal Sakyamuni is called the Original Buddha (*Hombutsu*), because he is the true form of the
Buddha. On the other hand, all kinds of limited Buddhas are
called duplicates, because they are traces or shadows reflect-
ing the true form. Buddhism believes in many Buddhas, but
they are all manifestations of the Original Sakyamuni Buddha.
In this way, all religious faiths are seen as one. Sakyamuni
continues:

> When I saw that some people of little virtue and much
> defilement were seeking the teachings of a lower level, I took
> a limited figure which was easier for them to understand, and
> then I appeared before them, telling them that I renounced
> my family when I was young, and attained Buddhahood.
> However, in reality, everlasting time (eternity) has passed
> since I became the Buddha. It is only to guide people that I

have been taking limited figures and expounding the law. All the sutras were expounded for this purpose, and for this purpose, I have been telling stories of my previous lives and the previous lives of other Buddhas, both in this and in other sutras. In some sutras, I manifested my duplicates, and in others, my transformations. In some sutras, I have described my own deeds, and in other sutras, the deeds of others. All that I say is true; it is never false. Because I see the "triple world" as it really is, I am never attached to illusions or see things in opposition or relatively, such as life and death, truth and falsehood, identity and differences. That is, seeing the relative world to be just that—relative, I am never attached to it.

People have such different dispositions that I expound various expedient teachings, such as parables and stories of previous lives, which I know will be understandable to each of them, and I have been leading people without rest for all eternity. I became the Buddha countless eons ago by practicing what I still practice—the Way of a Bodhisattva. The life span which I obtained has not yet expired. It is twice as long as previously stated (p. 243).

In this way, Sakyamuni announces that his life span is eternal. He is forever expounding the Dharma to save us all. In some other Buddhist scriptures, the Sanskrit term for the eternal Buddha is *Dharmakaya*, which is understood to mean that the truth itself is the Buddha. But the truth as an abstraction has no power to save us. Only when Sakyamuni realizes the truth in his person and activates the character of a Buddha in his practice does he become able to save us by the power of his mercy and wisdom.

The Lotus Sutra declares that the Buddha is immortal, existing eternally. This Buddha is called the Eternal and Original Sakyamuni Buddha. In contrast, the limited Sakyamuni, who renounced the world and attained Enlightenment at Buddha-gaya, is called, "the Buddha who attained Buddhahood at the city of Gaya," or simply the historical Buddha.

HISTORICAL IS ETERNAL

In Chapter Two, "Expedients," the Buddha revealed the three vehicles to be expedients—that is, provisional teachings. He clarified that the unity of the three in the One Buddha Vehicle is the true teaching. This is called "opening the provisional to reveal the truth," or "opening the three to reveal the one," or "the three teachings become one."

In this chapter, the "Duration of the Life of the Tathagata," it is explained that, while Sakyamuni is provisionally appearing in the limited figures of his manifestations, in reality, he is eternal and infinite. This is called "opening the near to reveal the distant," or "opening the provisional to reveal the truth," or similar expressions. Moreover, the first half of the Sutra, from Chapters One to Fourteen, is called Provisional, Imprinted, or Secondary (*Shakumon*), because Sakyamuni expounded it by means of his provisional duplicate; and the second half, from Chapter Fifteen to the final Chapter Twenty-eight, is called Original or Primary (*Hommon*), because Sakyamuni expounded it in the form of the Original Buddha (*Hombutsu*).

Sakyamuni continues:

Although I shall never enter Nirvana (extinction), I am here and now preaching that I shall. This is an expedient to save living beings. Why is that? Because if men and women of little virtue see me present here for a long time, they will neither appreciate me any longer nor plant good roots (for the future). On the contrary, they will become greedy and attached to their desires. If people see that I always exist and am immortal, they are satisfied and become neglectful. If they think they can see the Buddha any time they wish, they have no concept of how difficult it is to actually see a Buddha. Therefore, I use expedients, and preach that it is rare for a Buddha to appear in the world. In the long term, there is only one chance in many hundreds of billions of eons for living beings to personally meet a Buddha. Often there is no chance at all. So if I teach people that it is difficult to see a Buddha, they will realize that being able to listen to his words and see his form are, indeed, rare privileges. They will take advantage of such precious opportunities, and not squander them away. Therefore I preach that the Buddha enters Nirvana (p. 244).

This teaching tells a way of faith based on the subtleties of human nature. There is more than one way to understand and interpret the Buddha. However, for us ordinary people, he must be the One who relieves our worries and heals our pains right here in this world. This is his only real importance for us. (He must be able to help us now, not later; and here, not in some imaginary paradise.) We can compare the Buddha's method with that of parents, who raise their children with tender loving care. Most of the time, the children are not aware of how much is being done for them. They take their parents' love for granted. Often they fully appreciate all that their parents have done for them only after the parents have died. Then they wish they had displayed more gratitude when they had the chance. The parents, on the other hand, must be careful, and not give their children everything they ask for. Pampered children can quickly become spoiled and helpless. Their parents will not be able to care for them forever. Children must be trained to fend for themselves eventually, and not have to depend on their parents for everything.

Faith in the Buddha is like that. The Buddha preaches that he intentionally withholds his eternity from us until we are mature enough to appreciate it. In the meantime, he shows the phenomenon of Nirvana (here meaning extinction or death) to make us appreciate the value of faith.

The Buddha continues by giving another example of the relationship between parents and children. This is called the parable of "An Excellent Physician."

There was once an excellent and wise physician, who could cure all manner of diseases. He had many children. One day, while the physician was traveling in a distant part of the country, his children got into his medicine chest and began to sample what they found there. They liked the contents of one bottle in particular, and too late they realized that it was poisonous. They fell to the floor, writhing in agony.

Fortunately, the father returned home soon afterwards. He was shocked to find them in so much pain. "Father," some of them told him, "we drank from this bottle by mistake. Please do something to save us!" Others of the children only glared at him, as if it were all his fault in the first place. Some were already delirious, and could do nothing but moan.

The father knew exactly what to do. He went into his laboratory and mixed several ingredients to make a remedy. Then he brought it in and offered it to the children. Some took it immediately and were cured. Others had to be forced to take it. Still others refused to take it at all.

Then the father decided on an expedient. The obedient children, he knew, would take the remedy because he told them to. The disobedient children, on the other hand, would take it only if they wanted to, themselves. He set the remedy down nearby.

"There is nothing more I can do for you," he told them. "I must leave now on urgent business. Take this remedy I have prepared, and you will cure yourselves." Then he left them. A few days later, he sent a messenger to the house with the news that their father would return no more; he had died in a distant country.

The children were much grieved to hear this report. Those who had been disobedient complained the loudest. "If our father had been here, he would not have let us suffer like this. Now he can help us no longer. He has left us with only these bottles containing what he said was a remedy for our pain." Then they realized the precariousness of their position. If they did not take this remedy immediately, they could die.

They all took the remedy, and in due time were cured just as the father had predicted. When the father learned that his children were well again, he returned home and met them in a joyous reunion (p. 244-5).

In this story, the physician, the children's father, is compared to the Buddha, and the children are like us, ordinary people. The father's fictitious death is like the Buddha's entrance into Nirvana. The children suffering from poison means that our life is afflicted by various worldly desires, the most basic of which are called the "three poisons" (greed, anger, and ignorance). We who writhe in agony but reject the Buddha's eternal existence, are like delirious children. Only when he has left us, and we have found no other remedy, will we accept the remedy which he has left behind for us to take. And only after we have taken it in faith, does he reveal himself to us in his glorious reality.

We can comprehend this as a theory, or understand in our minds what is meant by the Eternal Buddha, but still not have faith in him. We can understand Buddhism, but still not realize its power. Only when we believe in him, can we actually see the Buddha.

Sakyamuni now repeats the chapter's central message in verses. These verses comprise the best known lines in all the Sutra. In Japanese, they are called *Jigage*, the "verses of eternity." Here are a few of them:

Since I became Buddha,
The time that has passed,
Has been immeasurable—
Hundreds of thousands of myriads
of incalculable kalpas (p. 246).

"Immeasurable" in this case is the same as "infinite." The time span has neither beginning nor end.

When people see me
Seemingly pass away,
Make offerings to my relics,
Adore me, admire me, become devout,
Upright and gentle,
And wish to see me

With all their hearts
At the cost of their lives . . . (p. 246)

As we mentioned before, we can see the real figure of
the Buddha when we devote ourselves to him in faith. We
can attain this faithful state when we devote both our body
and our soul to the Buddha and become unselfish. In other
words, we reach a state in which our hearts are completely
honest and gentle, and we leave all our cares in the hands of
the Buddha. A simple fervent feeling of entrusting one's life
to the Buddha is the essence of faith. In the words of the
sutra, we "wish to see (him) with all our hearts, and at the
cost of our lives."

In reality this world of mine is peaceful.
It is filled with gods and men.
Its gardens, forests, and palaces
Are adorned with all kinds of treasures.
Jewel trees blossom with flowers and fruit;
Sentient beings are joyful here;
Deities beat heavenly drums,
Make various kinds of music,
And rain mandarava-flowers on me
And all my assembly (p. 247-248).

This part implies that this very World of Endurance in
which we now live transforms into the Buddha's Pure Land,
where there is neither fear nor impurity. The words about
heavenly beings, gardens, forests, palaces, treasures, treasure
trees, and so forth, express the beauty and wonders of the
Pure Land.

Saha-world can be translated as "World of Endurance"
or "Perseverance." It is also called "the defiled land." Land of
Endurance means the place where we must bear up under
many pains, and "defiled land" means a place that is corrupted. When we humbly examine our conscience, we realize how many worldly desires we have, and how deeply we

have been contaminated by them. This is the normal human condition, so the real world, where such contaminated humans congregate, is filled with vice and impurity. Therefore, it is called the defiled land. On the other hand, we can imagine a Pure Land, created and inhabited by ideal beings. Such an ideal world, however, is generally thought to exist somewhere far away, infinitely distant from the real world. For example, the Western Pure Land of Amitayus Buddha, said to exist ten thousand billion countries to the west, is a typical expression of this human longing for a pure place somewhere where everyone will be happy.

However, it is important that the Pure Land should not be thought of as some far away place. It should be manifested right here. Ideas can be realized (made real) only by us, the people of this world. Here in the Lotus Sutra, it is taught that the Pure Land should be realized in this Saha-world. An important teaching of the Lotus Sutra is that "the World of Endurance is itself the Pure Land."

> This pure world of mine
> Can never be destroyed.
> My pure land is indestructible,
> But perverted people think:
> "It is full of sorrow, fear, and pain.
> It will soon burn away" (p. 248).

Because the Original Buddha is eternal and immortal, the Pure Land in this World of Endurance, where the Buddha lives, is also eternal and immortal. It can never be destroyed. However, we ordinary people, deluded by worldly desires and unable to see through the pure eyes of the Buddha, think that the World of Endurance is a defiled land, one which will finally burn away. We see this world as either incinerated by the sun, burned by hellfire, or consumed by worldly desires. We find ourselves in a hostile environment, where the forces of nature seek only to destroy us. We see grief, pain, and fear everywhere we look. To us, this is the "real world." Because of our corrupted hearts, this world, which should be a paradise, is utter defilement. It is this world, however, which our Buddha-nature can transfigure and realize in all its original glory.

The Buddha concludes by saying:

> I am always thinking:
> How can I cause all living beings
> To enter the supreme way
> And quickly become Buddhas? (p. 249)

These are the final words of the verses of eternity. The verses themselves are a summary of the entire chapter. These final words represent the deepest desire of the Buddha: his innermost heart of compassion. Ordinary people see the world as a defiled land, but the Buddha leads such people and saves them from the agonies of defilement, transforming their concept of reality as a lotus rises above the muddy water. And just as the Buddha's life span is eternal, so also is his yearning to save all beings from sufferings. "I am always thinking . . ." is his eternal wish. "The supreme way" is perfect enlightenment, and that means the same enlightenment which he himself enjoys—the enlightenment of a Buddha, which is to say, omniscience and its accompanying omnipotence. He concludes by desiring that all of us "quickly become Buddhas," and attain this highest state for ourselves.

In Chapter Two, "Expedients," the Buddha taught that his purpose in this world is to cause all people to open the treasury of the wisdom of the Buddha and for them to be shown, attain, and enter into this treasury. The Buddha Wisdom, of course, is the Buddha's enlightenment; so this is the same as causing people to attain enlightenment. The teachings which have been developed since Chapter Two are now expressed in terms of Sakyamuni's deepest and most heartfelt desire. This chapter's final words show the Buddha's hope that all living beings will attain the same Buddhahood which he himself enjoys.

To cause all people to attain Buddhahood; to direct them all to the one Buddha-world; and to establish Paradise in this actual world of ours, so that absolute individual peace of mind and absolute peace of society are realized. These are the great purposes of the teachings of the Lotus Sutra.

The Sutra of the Lotus Flower of the Wonderful Law

CHAPTER XVII: THE VARIETY OF MERITS

(The Assembly in the Sky)

The previous chapter, "The Duration of the Life of the Tathagata," explained that the Buddha's life span is eternal. This teaching is the most important of the Lotus Sutra. Therefore, the merits or benefits which the teaching brings us must be immeasurably great. That indeed is the case. This chapter, the "Variety of Merits," minutely delineates the benefits coming to anyone who hears Chapter Sixteen and accepts it by faith. The "variety" referred to means classifying and explaining those benefits in detail.

Sakyamuni begins by giving Maitreya many examples of Bodhisattvas who have attained merits by hearing about the Buddha's life span, and which stages of accomplishment they have attained. For example:

> Some Bodhisattvas attained the level of irrevocability (never falling back). Others will attain Buddhahood after they have experienced eight more lives. Others will attain Buddhahood after two lives, others after one life. . . . (p. 250-251).

> When Sakyamuni said these words, mandarava flowers and great mandarava flowers fell from the sky onto him and Many-Treasures Buddha in the Stupa of Treasures, and also onto the manifestations of Sakyamuni Buddha, who were seated beneath the trees on lion-thrones. Perfume and lovely music floated through the air. Bodhisattvas joined together in singing verses, their exquisite voices praising all the Buddhas (p. 251).

143

Sakyamuni Buddha continues teaching Maitreya about benefits which one can obtain after hearing the chapter, "The Duration of the Life of the Tathagata." He explains how practitioners of the Dharma, even those who have just begun to practice, should believe and accept this Sutra, and what merits they will obtain. This is called the "Four Faiths in the Present and the Five Stages in the Future," or the "Four Faiths and the Five Stages," and has long been considered an important teaching. "The present" means the present then, when Sakyamuni was in this world, and not our present today. At that time, there were four stages in the ideal method of faith and practice for his disciples. "The future" means after Sakyamuni has passed away, which is to say, our present and future. Now there are five levels or stages for practitioners of the Lotus Sutra. The names, "four faiths and five stages," are not found in the Sutra itself. Great Master Chih-i discerned them in this chapter, named them, and spoke about them in his book, *The Words of the Sutra of the Lotus Flower of the Wonderful Law*. His analysis has stood the test of time, and we should examine it further.

The Four Faiths in the Present mean four steps of belief: "Understanding by Faith in a Single Moment's Thought, Understanding the Meaning, Disseminating it to Others, and Entering into Deep Faith."

1. *Understanding by Faith in a Single Moment's Thought.*
As a first step, if anyone opens the heart in faith and understands the gist of the Sutra, even for just a moment, his or her happiness and virtue will be everlasting (p. 254-255).

2. *Understanding the Meaning.*
In the next step, one becomes clearly aware of the inner meaning of the Sutra.

3. *Disseminating it to Others.*
In the third step, one's practice makes further progress. The practitioner upholds and copies the Lotus Sutra, not only for

personal satisfaction, but also for the sake of others, expounding it to them, and having them copy it, too, or make offerings to it (p. 257).

4. *Entering into Deep Faith.*

At the fourth step, the practitioner mentally sees clearly the figure of the Original Buddha and his Pure Land and is able to enter into the state of deep faith, thanks to the teaching of the "Duration of the Life of the Tathagata" (p. 258).

At each of these steps, the benefits which we gain are boundless. In particular, Sakyamuni describes the great merit to be gained from taking the first step, "Understanding by Faith in a Single Moment's Thought." He says that the merits which Bodhisattvas gain by practicing the five perfections (*Paramitas*) , which consist of generosity, morality, patience, effort, and meditation, are indeed great. However, when compared to the benefits of Understanding by Faith in a Single Moment's Thought, all those merits are not equal to a hundredth, a thousandth, a hundred thousand myriadth of a *koti* of the merits for Understanding by Faith in a Single Moment's Thought. These five perfections are the same as the well-known "Six Perfections," minus the sixth and culminating one, the Perfection of Wisdom. To have faith in a single moment's thought when hearing the Buddha's deepest teaching, even if it is just a tiny bit, is an incomparably precious venture of the heart. Its merit is equal to that of the Perfection of Wisdom (which it achieves at one stroke). It is equal to the wisdom of the Buddha.

The five stages in the future consist of rejoicing on hearing the Sutra, reading and reciting the Sutra, expounding it to others, practicing the Six Perfections, and mastering the Six Perfections.

1. *The Stage of Rejoicing.*

At the first stage, one listens to the Lotus Sutra, receives it joyfully, and desires to follow its teachings (p. 258).

2. *The Stage of Reading and Reciting.*
At this stage, one who has already experienced the joy makes
further progress. He or she keeps the Lotus Sutra; reads and
recites it aloud, plumbs its meaning, and studies it more deeply.

3. *The Stage of Expounding It to Others.*
At this stage, one makes further progress yet, and is able to
explain the Sutra to others.

4. *The Stage of Practicing the Six Perfections (Paramitas).*
At this stage, one is so immersed in the Sutra that he or she
begins to practice the Six Perfections of a Bodhisattva.

5. *The Stage of Mastering the Six Perfections.*
At this final stage, one upholds the Lotus Sutra, plumbs its
deep meaning, explains it to others, practices the Six Perfections, and begins to realize them naturally in daily life.

The Six Perfections, which are mentioned above, are
considered to be the fundamental practices of Mahayana
Buddhism, the Great Vehicle, and are the Way of Bodhisattva
Practice. Their Sanskrit name, *Paramita,* really means,
"reaching the other shore." In other words, these are six
methods for attaining the goal of Buddhahood. The Six Perfections are:

I. *The Perfection of Generosity (dana-paramita, "giving").*
It has two meanings: giving material goods and giving
spiritual teachings. The Perfection of Generosity is the purest
manifestation of devoted service for others. This Perfection is
placed at the head of all others, for it summarizes the whole
spirit of the Great Vehicle.

II. *The Perfection of Morality (sila-paramita,* following the
ethical precepts).
There are five moral precepts in Buddhism, which are
considered to be aspirations, not commandments: (1) not to

take life, (2) not to steal, (3) not to indulge in unlawful sexuality, (4) not to lie, and (5) not to become intoxicated by drink or drugs.

III. *The Perfection of Patience (ksanti-paramita).*

When a Bodhisattva practices the Six Perfections, he is sure to encounter obstacles and opposition from other people. The Bodhisattva must remain patient in adversity. It takes courage sometimes to exercise self-control, not become angry, and not strike back with a blow for a blow.

IV. *The Perfection of Vigor (virya-paramita, "endeavor").*

Putting forth one's best effort. The final aim of the Perfection of Endeavor is to attain Buddhahood. We must approach every task with vigor and enthusiasm, and so improve our lives and the lives of those around us. No detail is too small not to require our best effort. The one great task of achieving Buddhahood requires the fulfilling of a thousand small tasks every day.

V. *The Perfection of Concentration (dhyana-paramita, meditation).*

Dhyana is called *Zen* in Japanese. It is sometimes translated as "Meditation," but in Buddhism there are various types of meditation, depending on what the one who meditates hopes to achieve. Here it means one-pointed concentration, not only of the mind but also of the heart. Any practice which helps us gain unity of mind and heart is dhyana.

VI. *The Perfection of Wisdom (prajna-paramita).*

The last of the Six Perfections is *Prajna*. It is the cornerstone of all the Perfections, for without Wisdom none of the others fit together. Without wisdom, none would be "perfections." Wisdom is not the same as simple knowledge or understanding. When the Buddha recognizes the truth (the Dharma), that is wisdom. In wisdom, the Buddha's person and the universal law (Dharma) are one. The state in which

subjective character and objective truth merge into one is true
wisdom.

This is the Buddha's wisdom, but we ordinary people
can obtain it also. For example, parents may know many
things about their children. No matter how much they know,
however, it is still just knowledge, not wisdom. It can be re-
placed by more or better knowledge, or it can be forgotten.
But when parents unite spiritually with their children, making
the children's hearts their own, and seeing the world through
the eyes of their children, then they truly know their children.
This way of knowing people and things by empathy is wisdom. It can neither increase nor decrease.

WISDOM

The Five Stages or Categories for the future, which we
have been discussing, show us what practitioners of the Lotus
Sutra should do once Sakyamuni has entered into Nirvana
and is no longer physically present among us. These five categories for practice in the future are quite similar to the four
faiths in the present, which we discussed previously. Both
imply a lifetime of effort and hard work on the long road to
perfection. (We might even find them discouraging; "nobody
is perfect.") But before dismissing them as impossible to fulfill, we should note again that both begin with the same first
step, that of joyfully accepting the message of eternal life in
Chapter Sixteen. Then gradually the practitioner begins to
read and discern the deeper meaning of the Sutra, finally becoming a teacher of it.

Concerning the first stages of "Rejoicing" and "Reading
and Reciting," Sakyamuni goes into some detail:

> The good men or women, who do not speak ill of this Sutra
> but really rejoice at hearing it after my extinction, should be
> considered to have already understood my longevity by firm
> faith. Needless to say, this is also true of those who read,
> recite, and keep it. Such persons should be considered to be
> carrying me on their heads. Ajita! They do not need to build a
> stupa or a monastery in my honor, or make the four kinds of

offerings to the Sangha, because those who keep, read, and recite this Sutra should be considered to have already built a stupa or a monastery, and to have made offerings to the Sangha. They should be considered to have already erected a wonderful and magnificent stupa of the seven treasures, and to have already equipped the stupa with all kinds of ornaments, and to have been doing so for many thousands of billions of eons (p. 258).

The Sutra says that, of course, building splendid stupas and temples, or contributing monetary donations and treasures to the Sangha produce many merits, because such deeds are evidence of a faithful heart. But compared to them, the merit which one obtains by keeping and practicing the Lotus Sutra is much more. It is true that there are stages in the practice of keeping the Sutra, as we have seen. But among those stages, the first one—having a joyful heart when one hears the Sutra—has the most significant meaning. Likewise, in the "Four Faiths in the Present," which we discussed first, "Understanding by Faith in a Single Moment's Thought" is mentioned first. It is only thanks to the faith and joy occurring within us the first time we grasp the meaning of the Lotus Sutra that we decide to practice it, act according to it, and finally attain enlightenment.

Nichiren considered these teachings of the Four Faiths and Five Stages to be extremely important practices in the Lotus Sutra. We know this from his writing called *Shishin Gohon Sho*, ("Selection of the Four Faiths and Five Stages"). Nichiren also taught that Understanding by Faith in a Single Moment's Thought and the stage of Joy are the vital points of these teachings. If we ordinary people, or those who are just beginning to practice the Lotus Sutra, have faith and joy for a single moment upon hearing it, it becomes natural for our hearts to want to learn and practice more. Nichiren taught that believing, accepting, and chanting the Sacred Title of the Lotus Sutra (Odaimoku) is the proper practice for us ordinary people in this Age of Degeneration. It is a practical way for all people—beginners as well as adepts—to practice the Sutra, and by doing so, attain Buddhahood. Understanding by Faith in a Single Moment's Thought and Joyful Acceptance are the cornerstones of the Four Faiths and Five Stages.

The Sutra of the Lotus Flower of the Wonderful Law

CHAPTER XVIII: THE MERITS OF A PERSON WHO REJOICES AT HEARING THIS SUTRA

(*The Assembly in the Sky*)

In the previous chapter, "Variety of Merits," the Five Stages were taught as practices for devotees of the Lotus Sutra once the Buddha has entered into Nirvana. The first stage, "Joy," is called the most important practice of all. This chapter, "The Merits of a Person Who Rejoices at Hearing This Sutra," explains how great the merits of joy really are.

At the beginning of this chapter, Maitreya approaches Sakyamuni and asks, "World-Honored One, how many merits will be given to a person who rejoices at hearing this Sutra of the Lotus Flower of the Wonderful Law after your extinction?" Sakyamuni answers:

Ajita (Maitreya)! Suppose a monk, a nun, a man or woman of pure faith, or anyone, young or old, rejoices at hearing the Lotus Sutra in some assembly after my extinction. After leaving the assembly, they go to some other place, such as a monastery, a retired place, a city, a street, a town, or a village. There they expound this Dharma just as they have heard it to their father, mother, relative, or friend, as well as they are able to. Then another person, one who has heard the Sutra from them, rejoices, goes to some other place, and tells it to a third person. The third person also rejoices at hearing it, and teaches it to a fourth person. In this way, the Sutra is heard by a fiftieth person. I will tell you of the merits of the fiftieth good man or woman who rejoices at hearing this Sutra.

There are many kinds of living beings in this universe. Suppose a rich man were to give all the beings within his sphere of influence many wonderful things—treasures, palaces, and so forth—whatever they wished. After giving generously for eighty years, this great philanthropist thought, "I have given them many wonderful things according to their desires. By now they are old and decrepit. Their hair is gray and their faces are wrinkled. Soon they will all be dead. I must lead them quickly to the Buddha's Dharma."

Then he gathered them all together, expounded the law to them, and led them to the highest rank of enlightenment in the Lesser Vehicle, which is called arhatship. Do you think that the merits gained by this great philanthropist were many or not?

Maitreya, you think that his merits were many—immeasurable, limitless—because he gave so much to all those beings and even led them to arhatship, don't you? However, the merits of such a person are less than the merits of the fiftieth person who rejoices at hearing even a verse of the Lotus Sutra. The merits of this great philanthropist are less than a hundredth or a thousandth of the merits of the latter person. The superiority of the merits of the latter person to those of the philanthropist cannot be measured by any calculation. The merits of the fiftieth person are beyond measure. Needless to say, so are the merits of the first person who rejoices at hearing the Sutra in the assembly. His merits are immeasurable, limitless, and incomparable.

Furthermore, Ajita, anyone who goes to a monastery or temple in order to hear this Lotus Sutra, and hears it even for a moment while he is sitting there or standing, in his next life, he or she will be able to ascend in a heavenly vehicle to a heavenly palace. Anyone who, while sitting in the place where the law is taught, persuades a newcomer to sit down and listen too, and shares his seat with that person, by such merits will be able to share the throne of King Sakra in the next life, or of Heavenly-King-Brahman, or of a wheel-turning-holy-king. And also, anyone who says to another person, "Let us go and hear the Lotus Sutra," and causes that person to hear it, by such an act will be able to live with Bodhisattvas of outstanding ability in his next life. He, too, will be clever and wise. He will be healthy and handsome. He will be able to see the Buddhas, hear the law from them, and receive their teachings by faith in all his future existences.

Ajita, look! The merits of one who causes even a single person to go and hear the law are so many! There is no need to speak of all of the merits of someone who receives this sutra with an open heart, reads it, recites it, expounds it to multitudes, and lives according to its teachings (p. 263-66).

After giving this teaching, Sakyamuni repeats it in verses. These verses, called the "merits of the joy of the fiftieth person," have been popular down through the ages.

In the previous chapter, "Variety of Merits," the teaching called the Five Stages of the Future was presented. The five stages consisted of joyful acceptance of the Sutra, reading it and reciting it, passing it on to others, practicing the Six Perfections, and mastering the Six Perfections. The first of these was joy. In this chapter, joy appears once again. It speaks about the joy which one experiences upon grasping for the first time the significance of the Sutra. That moment of joy is decisive for one's faith, and has an immeasurable impact on all one's future activities. This is the main point of this chapter.

"Rejoicing" is the joy which one experiences when the significance of the Sutra first sinks in like a ray of light. When this ray of light first illuminates our soul, we have not yet undertaken any profound studies or done any difficult practices. But the merits of that first moment of joy are greater than those of any other practices we may undertake later. It is the hinge upon which everything else turns. This is the essential and most important point of this chapter. Faith is simple; it is also decisive.

At the same time, it shows us how great the power of the Lotus Sutra really is. Many sutras other than this one contain excellent teachings for Bodhisattvas of great ability and "hearers" who abandon the world and join monastic brotherhoods or sisterhoods. However, such sutras are not suitable for ordinary people like us who have no special vocation or ability. The Lotus Sutra is suitable not only for great Bodhisattvas and ascetic Sravakas, as we might expect. This is for ordinary people who have no special abilities. This is the one Sutra with the power to save everyone.

The Sutra of the Lotus Flower of the Wonderful Law

CHAPTER XIX: THE MERITS OF THE TEACHER OF THE LAW

(The Assembly in the Sky)

In the previous chapter, "Merits of a Person Who Rejoices at Hearing This Sutra," the merits acquired by those who have just begun practicing the teaching are emphasized. This chapter, on the other hand, "Merits of the Teachers of the Law," speaks about merits acquired by practitioners in general. It is assumed that a practitioner of the Sutra will also be a teacher of the Dharma.

In the Lotus Sutra, we often see the sentence, "You should keep, read, recite, expound, and copy this Sutra." These activities are called the Five Kinds of Practice for a Teacher of the Dharma.

To keep the Sutra is to steadily accept and uphold the Lotus Sutra in one's mind. To read the sutra means to peruse the Sutra and read it. To recite the Sutra means to recite it or portions of it by heart. To expound the Sutra means to interpret it and teach it to others. To copy the Sutra means to copy it by hand. Practitioners of the Lotus Sutra should undertake these five practices. They have two aspects: practice for one's self and practice for others. This chapter says that persons who endeavor to practice the Five Kinds of Practice will be rewarded with splendid merits of their six sense-organs of the eyes, ears, nose, tongue, body, and mind. Sakyamuni explains this to a great Bodhisattva by the name of Constant-Endeavor.

"Such people," he tells him, "will be able to adorn and purify their six sense-organs with these merits" (p. 269).

The six sense-organs mean all the functions of body and mind. Practitioners of the Lotus Sutra will be able to purify their body and mind by this five-fold practice and enter into a state close to enlightenment. It is called the "purification of the six sense-organs." Here is an outline of Sakyamuni's teaching on this subject:

Purification of the Sense of Sight: "The eyes given to them by their parents (that is, their natural physical eyes) will be purified. These good men and women will be able to see the whole world, down to the deepest hell and up to the highest heaven. They will also be able to see all living beings of the world, know the karmas under which they now labor, and where those karmas will take them in the future" (p. 269).

Purification of the Sense of Hearing: "The ears given to them by their parents will be purified. They will be able to recognize voices and sounds of the whole world. They will be able to recognize the voices of monks, nuns, and Bodhisattvas who read and recite the Sutra and expound it to others. They will also be able to recognize the voices of Buddhas who teach all living beings and expound the Wonderful Law in great congregations" (p. 271-2).

Purification of the Sense of Smell: "The nose of this person will be purified. He or she will be able to know the smells of all things, be they good or evil, locate anything by smell, know by smell what people are thinking, and locate and discern where practitioners are and what they are practicing" (p. 274-8).

Purification of the Sense of Taste: "Their tongues will be purified. Anything tasting either good or bad will not be distasteful when put on their tongues, but will become as delicious as heavenly nectar. When they expound the law to the great multitude, they will be able to raise deep and wonderful

voices, making their message reach the hearts of their audience, and making the hearers become happy and cheerful.
All kinds of beings, even angels and heavenly maidens, will
come to them and make offerings to them in order to hear the
Dharma from them. Buddhas, Bodhisattvas, and sravakas will
also come to see them" (p. 278-9).

(5) *Purification of the Sense of Touch*: "The person's body will
become as pure as lapis lazuli. All living beings will want to
behold such a person. Just as a reflection is seen in a pure
mirror, so all things in the world, even the Buddhas and
Bodhisattvas expounding the law, will be reflected in the
pure body of that person" (p. 281).

(6) *Purification of the Mind*: "Their minds will become pure.
When they hear even a word or a verse of the Sutra with their
pure minds, they will be able to understand the innumerable
meanings of the Lotus Sutra. Any other teachings they expound will be consistent with the meanings of this Sutra and
not contrary to the reality of all things. If they expound the
scriptures of non-Buddhists, or give advice to the government, or teach ways to earn a livelihood, they will always be
in accord with the right teachings of the Buddha. Whatever
they think, measure, or say will be true, consistent not only
with these teachings, but also with the teachings that other
Buddhas have already expounded in the past" (p. 282).

These are the teachings of the purification of the six
sense-organs. Especially important are the words in the section on purification of the mind: "When they expound the
scriptures of non-Buddhists, or give advice to the government, or teach ways to earn a livelihood, they will always be
in accord with the right teachings of the Buddha." "To give
advice to the government" means to enter into the realm of
politics and administration. "To teach ways to earn a livelihood" refers to the realms of industry, economics, and our
daily work. Theories of politics and economics belong to the

ever-changing secular world. Buddhism, on the other hand, belongs to the eternal world, which lies beneath the transitory. Buddhist teachings and the common law (social rules) are distinct and should not be confused with each other. However, in the teachings of the Lotus Sutra, the Dharma cannot ignore the rules of society. On the contrary, the Dharma (truth) is the basis for social rules. Human society cannot function properly, even in politics or economics, unless it is in accord with the basic law of the universe. This law is what is meant by Dharma.

This is an important teaching of the Lotus Sutra. In his treatise *Kanjin Honzon Sho*, "Spiritual Contemplation of the Most-Venerable-One," Nichiren says, "One who understands the Law-Flower (the Lotus Sutra) can see the reasons for occurrences in the world."

The Sutra of the Lotus Flower of the Wonderful Law

CHAPTER XX: NEVER-DESPISING BODHISATTVA

(The Assembly in the Sky)

In this chapter, "Never-Despising Bodhisattva," Sakyamuni continues instructing the great Bodhisattvas. This time he addresses one by the name of Great-Power-Obtainer (Mahasthamaprapta).

> A long time ago, there lived a Buddha called Powerful-Voice-King Tathagata, who expounded the law for people for many years before he finally entered into Nirvana. After him, other Buddhas of the same name appeared one after the other—two billion altogether. After the last of these Buddhas, during the age of his counterfeit teachings, there lived many arrogant monks. These arrogant monks were influential and powerful. At the same time, there lived a Bodhisattva named Never-Despising. Whenever this Bodhisattva would meet people, he would bow to them in veneration, saying, "I deeply respect you. I do not despise you. Why? Because someday you will practice the Way of Bodhisattvas and all become Buddhas!"
>
> This Bodhisattva never read sutras or recited them. He just went up to people, bowed before them respectfully, and praised them, repeating, "I do not despise you, because you can become a Buddha." For this reason he was known as "Never-Despising" (p. 286).

The terms, "Age of Right Teachings" and "Age of Counterfeit Teachings," express the Buddhist view of history. It is

159

believed that for a while after a Buddha has entered Nirvana, people will remember his teachings correctly, put them into practice, and attain enlightenment. However, as time passes, those teachings will become mere academic formalities. People will know about them and be able to discuss them, but they will no longer practice them diligently and attain enlightenment. This second period is called the Age of Counterfeit Teachings. Finally, the teachings will decay altogether. People will neither practice them, understand them, nor attain enlightenment. This is the Age of Degeneration, when Buddhism declines and finally fades away. It is believed by most scholars that the first and second periods last for a thousand years each. The Age of Degeneration can drag on for as long as 10,000 years. In any case, Never-Despising Bodhisattva lived during the second of these three periods, an Age of Counterfeit Teachings.

> People resented Never-Despising for bowing to them, mistaking his humility for arrogance. They became angry and insulted him, saying, "Where did this ignorant monk come from? He has the nerve to say that he does not despise us, and assures us that we will become Buddhas. We don't need his false assurance of our future Buddhahood!" They threw stones at him, beat him with sticks, and persecuted him. But Never-Despising would just run away and shout at them from a distance, "I do not despise you, because you all will become Buddhas!"
>
> Those who inflicted persecutions on Never-Despising were mostly arrogant and conceited priests, who thought they had already attained what they actually had not. Never-Despising, on his part, never gave up, despite abuse and persecution. He spent his life bowing respectfully to everyone he met, praising them, and giving them his message of good will. When he was about to pass away, he heard a voice in the sky reciting the words of the Lotus Sutra, which had been expounded by the Powerful-Voice-King Buddha. He took these words to heart, and was able to purify his six senses (p. 286-7).

Purification of the six senses, which we discussed in the previous chapter, "Merits of the Teacher of the Law," means purification of the bodily senses of sight, hearing, smell, taste, touch, and mind. Once Never-Despising had purified his six senses, he was able to extend his lifetime for many years, and teach the Sutra to others. Thanks to his teaching, the same arrogant and conceited priests who had persecuted him before, now came to believe in the Lotus Sutra, themselves. In this way, he led many people to supreme enlightenment, and he himself became a Buddha.

"Who do you think this Bodhisattva was?" asked Sakyamuni. "As a matter of fact, the Never-Despising of that time was none other than myself. Those arrogant people who used to abuse Never-Despising fell into hell after their lifetimes and suffered fearful retribution. Afterwards they heard the Lotus Sutra from Never-Despising, and were enabled to aspire to the Buddha's enlightenment. One thousand five hundred of the Bodhisattvas, monks, and other people, who are now right here among us in this congregation, are the same people who once inflicted pain on Never-Despising" (p. 288).

This story of Never-Despising Bodhisattva shows the spirit which lies at the heart of the Lotus Sutra: respect for all human beings.

Human history and culture have long sought an ideal society composed of ideal persons. The Buddha, who is revealed in Buddhism, expresses this image of an ideal human being—omniscient, omnipotent, and magnanimous to all. The ideal society is his Pure Land. Not only Buddhism, but all religions seek such an ideal.

In our modern age, however, many people think that revolutions in politics and economics, instead of religion, are the best ways to realize such an ideal. "Liberty, Equality, and Fraternity," acclaimed in the French Revolution, express this spirit, although it soon came to mean liberty, equality, and fraternity for us, but not for you. In the twentieth century, the

Communist Revolution tried to realize the same ideal, also by brute force.

However, no such attempt can succeed without the spirit of Never-Despising Bodhisattva—venerating all living beings just as they are. This has been demonstrated by the recent collapse of communist countries in the former Soviet Union and eastern Europe. Although they had high ideals, their revolution, which ignored the value of human beings, was doomed to fail. Never-Despising Bodhisattva teaches the most basic revolution of all: profound respect for each and every living person.

The Sutra of the Lotus Flower of the Wonderful Law

CHAPTER XXI: THE SUPERNATURAL POWERS OF THE TATHAGATAS

(The Assembly in the Sky)

In Chapter Fifteen, the "Appearance of Bodhisattvas from Underground," the earth split open before Sakyamuni, and countless Bodhisattvas welled forth. Among these Bodhisattvas, four of them were the leaders. Their names were Superb-Action, Limitless-Action, Pure-Action, and Steadily-Established Action. They and the innumerable great beings accompanying them had appeared in this world to take on the task of disseminating the Lotus Sutra after Sakyamuni's extinction. In this chapter, "Supernatural Powers of the Tathagatas," Sakyamuni assigns them the mission for which they had come, and transmits the Sutra to them for dissemination in the future.

As the chapter begins, the Great Bodhisattvas from Underground offer to carry out Sakyamuni's assignment.

"After your extinction," they say, "we will expound the Wonderful Law for you." Thereupon Sakyamuni displays great supernatural powers in the presence of the assembled congregation headed by Manjusri. He emits rays of light from his body and illumines the worlds in all directions. The many manifestations of the Buddha, who are sitting on lion-thrones under jeweled trees, also emit rays of light from their bodies. They display their supernatural powers for one hundred thousand years.

Then Sakyamuni and his emanated Buddhas cough at the same time and snap their fingers. The sound of their simulta-

neous cough and finger-snapping reverberates over the Buddha-worlds in all directions, and the surfaces of those worlds
quake "in six ways." Living beings everywhere can see
Sakyamuni and Many-Treasures Buddha seated side by side in
the Stupa of Treasures. They can also see that many hundreds
of thousands of billions of Bodhisattvas and the four kinds of
devotees [monks, nuns, men, and women] are surrounding
the Two Buddhas respectfully. Perceiving all this, they are
delighted.

Everyone rejoices at seeing the whole cosmos transfigured
in this way. The congregation hears a voice from the sky saying, "Sakyamuni Buddha is now expounding the Sutra of the
Great Vehicle, which is called the Lotus Sutra. Let all living
beings rejoice! Bow down and make offerings to Sakyamuni
Buddha!"

Living beings from all directions join together in crying,
"Namah Sakyamuni Buddha! Namah Sakyamuni Buddha!
("Honor to Sakyamuni Buddha!") Then they strew flowers,
incense, and other precious things over the World of Endurance. The objects which they have thrown gather like billow-
ing clouds, transforming themselves into jeweled awnings ex-
tending over the entire World of Endurance. In the midst of all
this celestial glory, Sakyamuni transfers the Dharma to Superb-
Action and the other Bodhisattvas from Underground.

"The supernatural powers of the Buddhas are as immeasurable, limitless, and inconceivable as I have already told you. If
I were to speak for hundreds of thousands of billions of
asamkhyas of eons, I could not tell you all the merits which
will accrue to those to whom this Sutra is transmitted. To sum
up, (1) All the teachings of the Buddha, (2) all the unhindered
supernatural powers of the Buddha, (3) all the treasury of the
hidden core of the Buddha, and (4) all the profound achievements of the Buddha are revealed and expounded explicitly
in this Sutra. Therefore, after my extinction, you must keep,
read, and recite this Sutra, and act according to its teachings.
At any place where someone expounds this Sutra, or any
place where a copy of this Sutra is placed, be it in a garden, in

a forest, under a tree, in a monastery, in the house of a be-
liever, in a hall, on a mountain, in a valley, or in a wilderness,
there should a stupa be erected and offerings be made to it,
because that place is the Place of Enlightenment. Here the
Buddhas attained supreme-perfect-enlightenment. Here the
Buddhas turned the wheel of the Dharma. Here the Buddhas
entered into Parinirvana" (p. 292-294).

Sakyamuni's specially selected Bodhisattvas, headed by
Superb-Action, sprang up from underground. It is to them
that he transmits the Lotus Sutra. This transmission to the
Great Bodhisattvas is called the "Special Transmission" as
distinct from the "General Transmission," which will come
later.

We also find in these lines one of the special concepts of
the Sutra, namely, that a place where the Lotus Sutra is expounded is itself the Place of Enlightenment. This means that
anywhere we accept, believe, recite, and practice the Lotus
Sutra is the Place of Enlightenment. It is not necessary for us
to erect temples, fine buildings, or monuments in select holy
places.

What Sakyamuni transmits to Superb-Action and the
other Great Bodhisattvas, who welled up from underground,
is nothing less than (1) all the teachings of the Buddha, (2) all
the unhindered supernatural powers of the Buddha, (3) all
the treasury of the hidden core of the Buddha, and (4) all the
profound achievements of the Buddha. These are called the
Four Phrases of the Primary Mystery. Great Master Chih-i
taught that the meanings that the title (Daimoku) expresses—
that is, the meaning of the title itself, the purpose of the sutra,
its essential teachings, the influence it has upon its readers,
and the value of its teachings (which five he called the main
things to be commented on in interpreting any sutra)—are
expressed here in the Four Phrases of the Primary Mystery.
Nichiren, on the other hand, believed that the Four Phrases of
the Primary Mystery are to be found in the Sacred Title itself
(Odaimoku), and what Sakyamuni now transmits to Superb-

Action and the others is the Sacred Title of NAMU-MYOHO-
RENGE-KYO. ("I devote myself to the Sutra of the Lotus
Flower of the Wonderful Dharma.")

The chapter ends by repeating its main ideas in verses.
Here are some of them:

Anyone who keeps this sutra
Will be able to expound
The meanings of the teachings,
And the names and words [of this sutra].
His eloquence will be as boundless and unhindered
As the wind in the sky (p. 296).

Anyone who believes in and upholds the Lotus Sutra,
which is transmitted from Sakyamuni, has a thorough knowledge of the meanings of its diverse teachings, words, and
interpretations, and is able to expound them impartially, just
as the wind sails freely through the sky. That person will be
able to reach a stage of freedom, and remain there.

Anyone who understands why the Buddhas teach [many] sutras,
Who knows the position [of this sutra among the others],
And expounds it after my extinction,
According to its true meaning,
Will be able to eliminate the darkness
Of living beings in the world where he walks about,
Just as the light of the sun and the moon
Eliminates all darkness.
He will cause innumerable Bodhisattvas
To dwell firmly in the One Vehicle.

Therefore the man of wisdom,
Who hears the benefits of these merits,
And who keeps this sutra after my extinction,
Will be able to attain
The enlightenment of the Buddha
Definitely and beyond doubt.

These words were especially beloved by Nichiren. Needless to say, for him all the words of the Sutra were compelling. Nevertheless, he considered this chapter, the "Supernatural Powers of the Tathagatas," to be of singular importance. That is because it is here that Sakyamuni transmits the Four Phrases of the Primary Mystery, the essence of the Sutra, to Superb-Action and the Bodhisattvas from Underground. Nichiren believed that these Four Phrases are the Sacred Title (Odaimoku) of NAMU-MYOHO-RENGE-KYO. He maintained that in this chapter Sakyamuni calls the Bodhisattvas who had welled up from underground, headed by Superb-Action, and transmits to them the Sacred Title, the core of the Sutra manifested in its title. These Bodhisattvas, on their part, will appear in our times, the Age of Degeneration, to disseminate the Sacred Title and save all people, leading them to attain Buddhahood.

Nichiren compared his own position to that of Superb-Action Bodhisattva. After he was sent into exile on the Island of Sado, Nichiren began to make this comparison with increasing frequency. He stated it explicitly in his writing, *Kanjin Honzon Sho* ("A Treatise Revealing the Spiritual Contemplation of the Most-Venerable-One"). This essay is considered the most important of his many writings. Although its logical arguments resist condensation into a few words, here is a brief summary of what he said.

According to the teachings of Great Master Chih-i, the practical side of the Lotus Sutra is the doctrine of "one thought is the three thousand worlds" (ichinen-sanzen). However, if this doctrine is left in its original form, it is not a suitable practice for unenlightened people in this Age of Degeneration. If the theory of "one thought is the three thousand worlds" is followed through to its logical conclusion, it will be seen that the perfect Buddha resides in the hearts of unenlightened people. Then its realistic practice is clear. The effect attained by the Buddha's practice and all the virtues of his enlightenment are summed up and put into the five [Chinese] letters of the Sacred Title, MYO-HO-REN-GE-KYO

("The Sutra of the Lotus Flower of the Wonderful Law"). Sakyamuni transmitted it to everyone, the enlightened and the unenlightened, so that they might uphold and practice this Sacred Title (Daimoku).

According to the teachings of the Lotus Sutra, our World of Endurance is itself the eternal and everlasting Pure Land and this ever-existing and unchanging world of the Buddha exists in our own minds. This is taught in the Lotus Sutra, especially in the eight chapters, from Chapter Fifteen, the "Appearance of Bodhisattvas from Underground," to Chapter Twenty-two, "Transmission." It says in these eight chapters that Sakyamuni, who was seated in the Stupa of Treasures, summoned from beneath the earth countless Great Bodhisattvas headed by Superb-Action Bodhisattva. He transmitted to them the five letters of MYO-HO-REN-GE-KYO, which is the essence of the Lotus Sutra, and assigned them to disseminate it. The meaning of this decisive event is of fundamental significance. The scene of this transmission is the Most-Venerable-One (Honzon) and everyone should recognize it as such. All living beings should chant the Sacred Title of NAMU-MYO-HO-REN-GE-KYO and direct their veneration toward what is depicted here.

This Most-Venerable-One was revealed only in the Age of Degeneration. The Bodhisattvas from Underground did not appear during the Ages of Right Teaching and Counterfeit Teaching. They were assigned to appear here in our country, now in this Age of Degeneration. The Four Great Bodhisattvas, Superb-Action, Limitless-Action, Pure-Action, and Steadily-Established-Action, are the representatives of the Bodhisattvas who welled up from beneath the earth. They were told to come now, during the Age of Degeneration, disseminate the Sacred Title, and lead unenlightened living beings to Buddhahood.

Thus Nichiren maintains that the Bodhisattvas from Underground and their leaders, the Four Great Bodhisattvas, will appear in Japan during the Age of Degeneration. He discusses this in his essay, *Shoho Jisso Sho*, "The Reality of All

Things," saying that Bodhisattva Superb-Action, who was instructed by Sakyamuni to disseminate the Sutra in the future, has already come in the person of Nichiren himself:

> I, Nichiren, a man born in the Age of Degeneration, have nearly achieved the task of pioneering the propagation of the Wonderful Law, the task assigned to the Bodhisattva Superb-Action. . . . It is indeed too high an honor for me, a common mortal. . . . I, Nichiren, am the one who takes the lead of the Bodhisattvas from Underground. Then may I not be one of them? If I am one of them, why may not all my disciples and followers be their kinsmen? . . . If you are one in faith with Nichiren, you too are one of the Bodhisattvas from Underground.

The Sutra of the Lotus Flower of the Wonderful Law

CHAPTER XXII: TRANSMISSION

(The Assembly in the Sky)

After completing the special transmission [to the Great Bodhisattvas], as recorded in Chapter Twenty-one, "Supernatural Powers of the Tathagatas," Sakyamuni rises from his seat and extends his hands over the heads of [all the other] countless Bodhisattvas who have gathered there. He told them:

> For a time so long that it is beyond imagination, I practiced the law which is difficult to obtain, and attained supreme-perfect-enlightenment. I now entrust it all to you. Spread this teaching wholeheartedly after my extinction, and benefit and save all the people of the world (p. 297).

This is called the General Transmission, in which the Buddha entrusts his disciples to disseminate the Sutra after his departure. Three times he blesses his assembled followers, repeating the same words. Then he adds:

Because I have great compassion, I do not begrudge anything. I am fearless. I wish to give the Wisdom of the Buddha to all people. I am the great alms giver to all living beings. Follow me, and study my teachings. When you see good men or women, who believe in the Wisdom of the Buddha, you should teach them the Lotus Sutra. When you come across people who do not receive this Sutra by faith, you should show them some other profound teaching of mine, teach

them, and cause them to rejoice. That way you will be able to
repay all the favors you have received from the Buddhas
(p. 297-8).

After hearing these words, the Bodhisattvas were filled
with joy. With even more respect than they had shown
before, they bowed before him and repeated three times in
loud voices, "We will do as you command. Certainly, World-
Honored One! Please do not worry!"

After this, Sakyamuni instructed his manifestations to return in peace to their own worlds. So ends this brief chapter.
All the assembled beings, human and nonhuman, rejoiced
upon hearing it.

This is the teaching of Transmission. Here it is called the
General or Total Transmission, because by it the Lotus Sutra
is entrusted to all Bodhisattvas. What is the difference between this transmission and that which preceded it?

The Great Bodhisattvas from Underground, who received the Special Transmission in the previous chapter, are
called "Bodhisattvas Taught by the Original Buddha." They
are the direct disciples of the Eternal and Original Buddha,
who reveals his eternity and limitless true form in Chapter
Sixteen, "The Duration of the Life of the Tathagata." The other
Bodhisattvas, on the other hand, are called "Bodhisattvas
Taught by the Provisional Buddha." They are disciples of the
historical Buddha (the Provisional Buddha), whose figure is
limited and temporary. Among these Bodhisattvas, many are
representatives from other worlds.

Judging from the Sutra as a whole, we can see that the
Bodhisattvas Taught by the Original Buddha assume the duty
to disseminate the Lotus Sutra in the future, especially in the
Age of Degeneration. The Age of Degeneration in this defiled
World of Endurance will be filled with hazards and many
people will reject the Lotus Sutra and oppose its teachers.
Such a time and place will require Bodhisattvas of outstanding ability, ones who can overcome attitudes of apathy or
resentment. The Bodhisattvas taught by the Provisional

Buddha, on the other hand, are assigned a much easier task. They will work in this world during the Ages of Right Teaching and Counterfeit Teaching, or else in other worlds.

"Transmission" is a word meaning essentially delegation and trust. In Buddhist scriptures (sutras), after Sakyamuni has expounded a particular teaching, he always ends by entrusting it to certain listeners. They are told to practice what they have been taught and spread the teaching to others. This part of the sutra, which normally comes at the end, is called the transmission. Sometimes the transmission section is brief, consisting of no more than a few lines. Other times it makes up an entire chapter, as we see here in the chapter entitled, "Transmission." Nearly all sutras consist of three parts: an introduction, the principal teaching, and the transmission.

The Lotus Sutra, on the other hand, does not end with the transmission. This is only Chapter Twenty-two; more chapters are to follow until we reach the final Chapter Twenty-eight. This in itself makes it very different from other sutras. Does the positioning of the transmissions so far from the end of the book have some special meaning? Generally the transmission section, or transmission chapter, simply closes the book and has no particular significance. In this Sutra, on the other hand, we find it about half-way through the second and principal half of the Sutra, the Primary Mystery *(Hommon)*. Indeed, the transmission can be considered part of the main teaching of the Primary Section *(Hommon)*, and not just an addition. In other words, the main part of the Lotus Sutra tells how Sakyamuni transmits it to the Bodhisattvas, and then how the Bodhisattvas disseminate it and make it prevalent after his extinction.

Nor is that the only difference from the usual pattern of introduction, main body, and transmission. Beginning as early as Chapter Ten, "The Teacher of the Law," we find numerous references to disseminating the Sutra after the Buddha's extinction. Such references are found in no less than sixteen of the twenty-eight chapters, which is more than half the chapters in the book. Such a strong emphasis on

dissemination is unique in Buddhist literature, making it another special characteristic of the Lotus Sutra. To disseminate
the Sutra is an integral part of the main message.

The main practice of Mahayana Buddhism, the Great
Vehicle, is the Practice of a Bodhisattva: practice for helping
others. The sutras in general give us many types of
Bodhisattva-practices. In the Lotus Sutra, however, the principal Bodhisattva-practice is dissemination of the Sutra itself.

In Chapter Eleven, "Beholding the Stupa of Treasures,"
and Chapter Eighteen, "Encouragement for Keeping the
Sutra," Sakyamuni asks Bodhisattvas to volunteer to dissemi-
nate the Sutra in the future. Answering his call, in Chapter
Fifteen, "The Appearance of Bodhisattvas from Under-
ground," Bodhisattvas well up from beneath the earth,
and in Chapter Twenty-one, "Supernatural Powers of the
Tathagatas," Sakyamuni transmits the Sutra to them. Then in
Chapter Twenty-two, "Transmission," he transmits it to all the
Bodhisattvas. The mission of all of them, both the Original
Bodhisattvas and the Temporal Bodhisattvas, is to dissemi-
nate the Lotus Sutra after the Buddha's extinction.

A principal feature of the Lotus Sutra lies in showing us
spiritual and practical ways by which Bodhisattvas disseminate it, overcoming all hardships in this evil world.

The Sutra of the Lotus Flower of the Wonderful Law

CHAPTER XXIII: THE PREVIOUS LIFE OF MEDICINE-KING BODHISATTVA

(The Second Assembly on Mt. Sacred Eagle)

The story of Medicine-King Bodhisattva begins with an explanation of his accomplishments in a previous life. In Chapter Ten, the "Teacher of the Law," Medicine-King represented eighty thousand Bodhisattvas who heard Sakyamuni teach. In this chapter, Sakyamuni tells a Bodhisattva by the name of Star-King-Flower about the Medicine-King.

A long time ago, there was a Buddha called Sun-Moon-Pure-Bright-Virtue Tathagata. Among his many disciples, there was one named Gladly-Seen-By-All-Beings Bodhisattva. He studied the Lotus Sutra under this Buddha, and underwent difficult practices for many years until he attained the samadhi by which he could transform himself into any other living being (p. 299-300).

The samadhi by which he could transform himself into any other living being is the samadhi (the power of concentration) that is the ability to show an appropriate physical form according to the person's capacity to whom he preaches the dharma.

Gladly-Seen-By-All-Beings entered into deep meditation. The sky about him filled with falling flowers and the scent of sandalwood. He gathered up these celestial flowers and offered them to the Buddha. Nonetheless, he realized that such

175

offerings, wondrous as they were, were inferior to the offering of his own life. Therefore he drank various kinds of oil, poured sweet smelling oil over his body, and set himself on fire before the Buddha. The light of the flame emitted from his body illuminated the whole world.

This offering is called burning one's body. Gladly-Seen-By-All-Beings illuminated the world for twelve hundred years until his body was completely consumed.

Afterwards he was reborn as the son of a king named Pure-Virtue. One day he told his father about his previous existence and about how he had obtained the samadhi by which he could transform himself into any other living form. He went on to tell him how he had once given his own body as an offering, and that he wanted to make another offering to Sun-Moon-Pure-Bright-Virtue Buddha, who was still alive at the time.

After saying these things, he flew into the sky. He went to Sun-Moon-Pure-Bright-Virtue Buddha, performed a miracle, and made an offering before him. Sun-Moon-Pure-Bright-Virtue said to him, "I will enter Nirvana this very night. I transmit all my teachings, treasures, and relics to you. Erect stupas to enshrine them, and make offerings to them!"

After leaving these final instructions, Sun-Moon-Pure-Bright-Virtue Buddha entered into Nirvana. The king's son was overcome with sorrow. He gathered firewood made of candana birch, and cremated the body of the Buddha. Then he gathered the ashes and erected eighty-four thousand stupas in which to enshrine them. Finally, he sat down before the stupas, and for seventy-two thousand years burned his elbows as an offering to the Buddha.

When people saw the Bodhisattva lose his elbows, they felt sorry for him. But the Bodhisattva made a vow to them, saying, "Since I made an offering of my elbows, I will become a Buddha with a golden body if my words are true. Then my two elbows will be restored."

As he made the vow, his elbows were restored, and the whole universe quaked with joy. Flowers rained down from heaven, and the people were ecstatic (p. 300-304).

After telling this story about Gladly-Seen-By-All-Beings Bodhisattva, Sakyamuni explained its significance to Star-King-Flower Bodhisattva:

"Do you know," he asked, "who Gladly-Seen-By-All-Beings really is? He is none other than the present Medicine-King Bodhisattva. Anyone who wants to attain enlightenment can do so by burning just one finger or toe, and making an offering just like Medicine-King did in his former life. This kind of offering is more valuable than the offerings of lands, palaces, and treasures" (p. 304).

Sakyamuni continues to explain that the Lotus Sutra is unsurpassed by any other sutra. He gives ten metaphors of comparison: (1) just as the sea is larger than rivers; (2) just as Mt. Sumeru is the highest of all mountains; (3) just as the moon god is brighter than other living beings; (4) just as the sun god dispels all darkness; (5) just as the wheel-turning-holy-king is superior to ordinary monarchs; (6) just as King Sakra is king of the thirty-three gods; (7) just as the Great-Brahman-Heavenly-King is the father of all living beings; (8) just as a saint is superior to unenlightened mortals; (9) just as Bodhisattvas are superior to Sravakas or Pratyekabuddhas; (10) just as the Buddha is King of the Dharma; so the Lotus Sutra is king of all sutras.

What is more, the Lotus Sutra has the power to save all living beings from suffering and give them great joy:

This sutra saves all living beings. . . . This sutra saves them from all sufferings. . . . Just like a man who reaches a stream of fresh water when he is thirsty; just like a man who finds a fire when he is cold; just like a man who is given a garment when he is naked; just like a party of merchants who find a ship when they want to cross a river; just like a sick person who finds a skilled physician; just like a man who is given light when he is in darkness; just like a poor man who finds a treasure; just like the people of a nation who enthrone a new king; just like a trader who reaches the seacoast; just like a torch which dispels darkness; so this Sutra of the Lotus Flower of the Wonderful Law saves all living beings from sufferings, from diseases, and from the bonds of death (p. 305).

The chapter concludes by naming more virtuous deeds and countless merits, saying that the Lotus Sutra is the best medicine to cure the sickness of the world.

The offering of burning the body, which plays such a prominent part of this chapter, should not be taken literally. It symbolizes the spirit of giving one's whole self, believing wholeheartedly, embracing the Most-Venerable-One, and offering to serve the truth with all one's body and soul.

The Sutra of the Lotus Flower of the Wonderful Law

CHAPTER XXIV: WONDERFUL-VOICE BODHISATTVA

(The Second Assembly on Mt. Sacred Eagle)

As the chapter of Wonderful-Voice Bodhisattva begins, Sakyamuni emits a ray of light from the tuft of hair between his eyebrows. The light illumines the eastern worlds of the Buddhas.

This light passed a countless number of worlds and illuminated a world called Pure-Light-Adornment. In that illuminated world there lived a Buddha called Pure-Flower-Star-King-Wisdom Tathagata, who was expounding the law to a multitude of his disciples gathered about him respectfully. Among those disciples was a Bodhisattva named "Wonderful-Voice" (Gadgadasvara). This great Bodhisattva had accumulated many merits, served under numerous Buddhas, and attained various samadhis.

When the ray of light illuminated him, he went before Pure-Flower-Star-King-Wisdom and told him that he wished to visit the World of Endurance, meet Sakyamuni Buddha, and see Manjusri, Superb-Action, and the other great Bodhisattvas living there.

Pure-Flower-Star-King-Wisdom Buddha understood his wish, but told him, "Do not despise that world (the World of Endurance)! Do not consider it inferior to our world! That world is uneven. It is full of mountains, rocks, dirt, and impurities. The Buddha of that world and his Bodhisattvas are shorter in stature than we are. You are forty-two thousand yojanas tall (one yojana is about ten miles), and I am six million eight hundred thousand yojanas tall. You are handsome and illuminated by many meritorious attributes. Your body glows beautifully. You may be tempted to feel superior to those [miserable creatures] who live there. However, be careful not to denigrate them or the world in which they live.

Wonderful-Voice said that he understood. He then concentrated his mental faculties and entered into samadhi. Suddenly eighty-four thousand lotus flowers appeared around Mount Sacred Eagle in the World of Endurance, where Sakyamuni was. These noble beautiful flowers had golden stems, silver leaves, diamond stamens, and gem calyxes.

On seeing the sudden appearance of the flowers, Manjusri asked Sakyamuni, "What is the meaning of this omen?" Sakyamuni replied, "It is a sign that Wonderful-Voice Bodhisattva is coming from the World of Pure-Light-Adornment to make offerings to me and the Lotus Sutra." As this was the first time that Manjusri had ever heard of Wonderful-Voice Bodhisattva, he asked for more information about him. "Who is he? What kind of practice did he do to attain such powers? What does he look like and how does he act? I would love to see him."

Hearing this, Sakyamuni asked Many-Treasures to make Wonderful-Voice appear before them. Many-Treasures summoned him as Sakyamuni requested. Wonderful-Voice immediately appeared in the World of Endurance. He was accompanied by eighty-four thousand attendants.

All the worlds, through which these great beings had passed, quaked in six ways. Lotus flowers of the seven treasures fell from the skies, and beautiful melodies sounded in the air. The eyes of the Bodhisattva were like large blue lotus flowers, and his face was more handsome by hundreds of thousands of times than the light of the moon. His body shone like pure gold. His appearance was majestic and awe-inspiring. He was seated on a throne of seven treasures, which came through the sky and alighted in front of Sakyamuni

Buddha. The Bodhisattva got down from his throne, bowed before the Buddha's feet, and made offerings to him.

"Pure-Flower-Star-King-Wisdom, Buddha of the world Pure-Light-Adornment, sends you his greetings. He instructed me to inquire if you are in good health, if the worldly affairs here are endurable, if people are following your teachings, how is Many-Treasures Tathagata, and how long will he remain in the World of Endurance. I also would like to see Many-Treasures, myself" (p. 311-312).

Sakyamuni relayed this message to Many-Treasures, and praised Wonderful-Voice Bodhisattva for having come so far to make offerings to the Buddha and the Lotus Sutra.

Then a Bodhisattva named "Flower-Virtue" (Padmasri) approached the Buddha and asked, "What kind of practice in his previous lives did Wonderful-Voice do to obtain such supernatural powers?" Sakyamuni said in reply, "Long ago, there was a Buddha called Cloud-Thunder-Peal-King Tathagata; his world was known as Appearance-of-All-Worlds. Wonderful-Voice made many offerings of beautiful music to this Buddha. Because of his great deeds, he was able to be born in the world of Pure-Flower-Star-King-Wisdom Tathagata, and there he acquired supernatural powers. This is the Bodhisattva whom you see here now. He continued practicing and accumulating virtues until he was able to transform himself into thirty-four kinds of living beings, such as King Brahman, King Sakra, Freedom God (Isvara), a Brahmin priest, a man or woman of pure faith, a monk, a nun, a man, a woman, a boy, a girl, a god, a dragon, a yaksa, and so on. He changes into these forms in order to meet living beings at their own level, put them at ease, and teach them the Dharma."

Flower-Virtue Bodhisattva understood this. Then he asked, "What kind of practice is necessary to attain such supernatural powers?" Sakyamuni replied, "You should practice the samadhi by which you can transform yourself into various living beings. This is a very important practice. You can obtain this supernatural power if you thoroughly share the feelings

and aspirations of others, and that way you will be able to
save them" (p. 312-314).

Wonderful-Voice Bodhisattva finished making offerings
to Sakyamuni Buddha, and then returned to his own
world. There he reported to Pure-Flower-Star-King-Wisdom
Tathagata, told him he had made offerings in the World of
Endurance, and had taught the eighty-four thousand
Bodhisattvas accompanying him how to attain the samadhi to
transform themselves into various living beings.

This is an outline of the chapter, "Wonderful-Voice-
Bodhisattva," and we can see that it contains some interesting
teachings. Since the Saha-world we live in is filled with evil
and impurity, it is called "the defiled land." It is also called the
World of Forbearance or Endurance, because the living beings which dwell here endure many sufferings. An ideal
world, on the other hand, is called a Pure Land. Before the
Lotus Sutra was taught, it was believed that a Pure Land can
exist only somewhere else, somewhere far away from this
defiled land. One such Pure Land is mentioned in the Lotus
Sutra. It is the Western Paradise of Amitayus. However, the
Pure Land of the Lotus Sutra exists not only in the west, but
everywhere.

In this chapter, the Pure Land of Wonderful-Voice
Bodhisattva is described as existing in the east. According to
the Lotus Sutra, however, the Pure Land should not be anywhere else than right here in our Saha-world. This idea was
presented in Chapter Sixteen, the "Duration of the Life of the
Tathagata." It is a principal theme of the Lotus Sutra, which
always emphasizes practice in our real world. It concludes
that "the Saha-world itself is the Pure Land."

However, many Buddhists, who do not have a thorough
understanding of the Lotus Sutra, still think of the Pure Land
as being somewhere else, away from the Saha-world. The
Lotus Sutra accommodates this popular belief and differenti-
ates between the eastern Pure Land, the western Pure Land,
and the defiled land. This chapter of Wonderful-Voice-

Bodhisattva shows us that this World of Endurance is pivotal, however, no matter how inferior it may seem when compared to the pure lands of the east and west. It is here that people live and die. It is here that they conceive of pure lands existing either to their east or west. It is here that the Eternal Original Buddha reveals himself. It is here that the other Buddhas and Bodhisattvas come to pay homage. Thus Pure-Flower-Star-King-Wisdom Buddha warns Wonderful-Voice not to denigrate the World of Endurance. Its crucial importance belies its miserable outward appearance.

The samadhi by which one can transform himself into other living beings is a power of concentration acquired by practice. Such a miraculous phenomenon may sound impossible. However, when we sincerely devote ourselves to the service and welfare of others, we can reach a stage of non-self—real selflessness—and become one with them. In appearance, we may even look like one of them. An adult playing happily with children may look like a child himself. He may feel like a child, too. The children may even consider him to be one of them. Such "transformations" are far from impossible, but they do require a special state of mind. The samadhi by which one can transform himself into other living things is an expression of the Bodhisattva-spirit of devoting one's self to others. Wonderful-Voice can transform himself into thirty-four bodies. In the next chapter, we meet a famous Bodhisattva with similar abilities.

The Sutra of the Lotus Flower of the Wonderful Law

CHAPTER XXV: THE UNIVERSAL GATE OF WORLD-VOICE-PERCEIVER BODHISATTVA

(The Second Assembly on Mt. Sacred Eagle)

Chapter Twenty-five, the "Universal Gate of World-Voice-Perceiver Bodhisattva," is often called the "Sutra" of World-Voice-Perceiver. This is because it is sometimes published and recited as an independent work, complete in itself. The Bodhisattva who appears in this chapter is the focus of a distinct cult, which relies on this chapter (or sutra) as its primary source.

What is the meaning of the name "World-Voice-Perceiver" (Avalokitesvara)? At the beginning of this chapter, a Bodhisattva named "Endless-Intent" (Aksayamati) asks Sakyamuni Buddha this very question.

> "World-Honored One, why is World-Voice-Perceiver called by that name?" The Buddha said to him, "Good man! If many hundreds of thousands of billions of living beings hear the name of World-Voice-Perceiver, and in times of troubles, wholeheartedly call his name, World-Voice-Perceiver will immediately perceive their voices, and cause them to free themselves from their sufferings" (p. 316).

In this world, we have many problems and sorrows, and since we are not able to overcome them ourselves, we complain about them loudly. When World-Voice-Perceiver hears our voices, he immediately discerns what our problem is, solves it, and leads us towards enlightenment. That is the

185

reason for his name. In Asia, millions of people chant his name sincerely for delivery from their troubles.

World-Voice-Perceiver, says Sakyamuni, can save us from seven calamities:

SEVEN
CALAMITIES

1. *The calamity of fire.* Those who keep the name of Avalokitesvara will not be burned even if they are trapped in a conflagration (p. 136).

2. *The calamity of water.* Those who call upon the name of World-Voice-Perceiver will be washed ashore if they are swept away by a flood.

3. *The calamity of raksasa demons.* Suppose people are crossing an ocean in search of a treasure, and their ship is tossed by a storm to a country of raksasa demons. If just one member of the ship's company calls upon the name of World-Voice-Perceiver, everyone on board will be saved.

4. *The calamity of swords and clubs.* If anyone is about to be struck by a sword or a club, and he calls on the name of Avalokitesvara, the sword or club will suddenly shatter into pieces.

5. *The calamity of yaksa demons.* If a host of yaksa or raksasa demons assault a person who calls upon the name of Avalokitesvara, they will not be able to harm him.

6. *The calamity of chains and shackles.* If anyone, guilty or not, calls the name of World-Voice-Perceiver when he is bound in chains and shackles, the chains will break, and he will be freed.

7. *The calamity of bandits.* Suppose the chief of a party of merchants is leading a richly laden caravan along a dangerous road haunted by many bandits. If all the members of that caravan call upon the name of World-Voice-Perceiver, they will not be attacked, but will pass by in safety.

This chapter says that if someone calls the name of this Bodhisattva, he or she will be able to avoid these seven calamities. Such benefits, by which one can avoid calamities and obtain happiness, are called "benefits in this world." The teachings of this chapter list many of them. However, to obtain such benefits, we must have pure hearts. The Buddha and the Bodhisattvas grant such benefits only to people who practice sincerely. The purpose of calling the name of World-Voice-Perceiver is really to show our sincerity to him. This is made clearer in the next lines, which mention basic virtues such as sincerity, patience, and wisdom.

Lustful persons will be relieved of lust if they think about Bodhisattva World-Voice-Perceiver. Angry people will calm down if they think about him and respect him. Perplexed people will acquire clarity of mind if they think of him and respect him (p. 317).

Lust, resentment, and stupidity are called the "three poisons" in Buddhism. They are sometimes translated as greed, anger, and ignorance. The seven calamities listed above are material and physical sufferings of human nature, and the three poisons are mental sufferings. Material sufferings come upon us because the mental sufferings exist already as their bases. If our suffering minds are healed of the three poisons, we can expect material calamities to disappear, too.

Endless-Intent Bodhisattva (Aksayamati) now asks Sakyamuni, "What expedients does World-Voice-Perceiver (Avalokitesvara) employ to expound the law in this world?" Answering this question, Sakyamuni says that World-Voice-Perceiver can transform himself into thirty-three different forms to save people. This is similar to the way Wonderful-Voice transforms himself into thirty-four bodies. However, there are a few differences between the two. World-Voice-Perceiver takes on any of the following thirty-three forms:

(1) a Buddha, (2) a Pratyekabuddha, (3) a Sravaka, (4) Heavenly-King-Brahman, (5) King Sakra, (6) Freedom God (Isvara), (7) Great-Freedom God (Mahesvara),

(8) a commander of heavenly hosts, (9) the god Vaisravana, (10) the king of a small country, (11) a rich man, (12) a householder, (13) a prime minister, (14) a Brahman [or Brahmin, a member of the highest Indian caste], (15) a monk, (16) a nun, (17) a man of pure faith, (18) a woman of pure faith, (19) the wife of a rich man, (20) the wife of a householder, (21) the wife of a prime minister, (22) the wife of a Brahman, (23) a boy or a girl, (24) a god, (25) a dragon, (26) a yaksa, (27) a gandharva, (28) an asura, (29) a garuda, (30) a kimnara, (31) a mahoraga, (32) a human or nonhuman being, and (33) the Vajra-holding God (p. 318-19).

Not only do all of us have different faces and forms, but also different beliefs and aspirations according to our race, nationality, occupation, social status, age, education, and so forth. A leader must understand people's feelings, and display an attitude and appearance that are harmonious with theirs. That is why this Bodhisattva transforms himself into other living beings. "Good man," says Sakyamuni, "In a certain world, World-Voice-Perceiver Bodhisattva takes the shape of a Buddha in order to save those who are to be saved by a Buddha. He takes the shape of Vajradhara [God of Power and Might] by those who are to be saved by Vajradhara" (p. 318-19).

In Chapter Two, "Expedients," the Buddha says, that although he has only one teaching (the One Vehicle), he divides it into several according to people's capacities. In this chapter, World-Voice-Perceiver Bodhisattva employs the same expedient, not by using words, but by using his many appearances.

The complete name of this chapter is the "Universal Gate of World-Voice-Perceiver Bodhisattva." Universal Gate means that he [or she], representing the gate of Buddhism, is open to everyone without exception. This does not mean that there is only one gate [as some religions teach]. There are as many gates as there are people and other creatures who are in need. Gate is mukha in Sanskrit, which also means "face" in that language. World-Voice-Perceiver has many faces, which means he is expounding many teachings.

An often asked question is whether World-Voice-Perceiver is male or female. Many people think she is female. [In Chinese, her name is translated as Kwan Yin, and she is frequently depicted as the gentle "Lady of Mercy."] That is not exactly correct, however. The true answer to the question depends on people's desires. If someone wishes to see a beautiful woman, the Bodhisattva looks like just such a woman to that person. If someone wants to see a great man [or a god], the Bodhisattva appears as such a man [or god]. World-Voice-Perceiver is neither masculine nor feminine, but either one or the other. He or she looks male or female depending on people's desires. Actually, in Sanskrit, all the Buddhas and Bodhisattvas have masculine names, and for that reason they are usually identified as male.

> Endless-Intent Bodhisattva was so impressed by what he heard about World-Voice-Perceiver that he wanted to make him an offering. He removed an invaluable necklace from around his neck and offered it to World-Voice-Perceiver as a token of his esteem, saying, "Please receive this necklace." However, World-Voice-Perceiver would not accept it. Seeing this, Sakyamuni told him, "Take it out of your pity for him and all the humans and nonhumans whom he represents." Then World-Voice-Perceiver agreed to accept it, but he did not keep it for himself. Instead, he divided it into two parts, offering one half to Sakyamuni and the other half to the stupa of Many-Treasures Buddha (p. 319-320).

The chapter ends with verses which repeat the same themes we have seen. Faith in World-Voice-Perceiver is widespread in Asia. Many beautiful works of art have depicted this popular Bodhisattva, sometimes showing her as female and sometimes as male. In English, she is often misnamed the "Goddess of Mercy." Among the many representations of Avalokitesvara, seven figures are particularly famous, and more especially, two of them: the "World-Voice-Perceiver of Eleven Faces," and "World-Voice-Perceiver of a Thousand

Hands." The thousand hands signify that World-Voice-Perceiver offers a multitude of gifts to our suffering world.

The perfect Bodhisattva shares the same heart with the Buddha, helping and saving countless humans and nonhumans by whatever means necessary for the occasion. Avalokitesvara, World-Voice-Perceiver, is the exemplar of the Bodhisattva-ideal.

The Sutra of the Lotus Flower of the Wonderful Law

CHAPTER XXVI: DHARANIS

(The Second Assembly on Mt. Sacred Eagle)

Dharani is a Sanskrit word; in Chinese it is taken to mean "total upholding." Total upholding means holding on to the good, thus preventing evil. Since it has the meaning of not to lose the [good] teachings of the Buddha, it signifies to memorize phrases of the Sutra. The memorized phrases of teachings are called dharanis, and phrases of spells are called dharani-ju or dharani-jinju. In this chapter of the Sutra, dharani refer to dharani-ju.

> Thereupon Medicine-King (Bhaisajyaraja) rose from his seat and asked Sakyamuni, "How many merits will be given to the good men or women who read and recite the Lotus Sutra?"
>
> Sakyamuni answered, "Suppose some good men or women make offerings to eight hundred billion nayuta Buddhas. The merits given to them are indeed many. However, even more merits will be given to the good men or women who keep, read, and recite even a phrase or a verse of the Sutra."
>
> Then Medicine-King said to the Buddha, "I will now give dharani-spells to expounders of the Lotus Sutra in order to protect them. These spells have already been expounded by billions of Buddhas. If there are people who attack or abuse a teacher who reads and recites the Lotus Sutra, they should be considered to have attacked and abused all those Buddhas."
>
> Then he uttered these dharani-spells: "Ani, mani, mane,

191

mamane, shire, sharite, shamya, shabitai, sente, mokute, mokutabi, shabi, aishabi, sobi, shabi, shae, ashae, agini, sentei . . ." (p. 325-326).

Next Brave-In-Giving Bodhisattva (Pradanasura) rose from his seat and said, "World-Honored One, I also will utter dharanis in order to protect anyone who reads, recites, and keeps the Lotus Sutra. If a teacher keeps these dharanis, he will not have his weak points exploited by any demon." Then he uttered these spells: "Zarei, makazarei, ukki, mokki, arei, arahatei, netsureite, netsureitahete" (p. 327).

Then Vaisravana Heavenly-King rose from his seat to contribute dharani-spells of his own. "World-Honored One, I will protect a teacher of the law with these divine spells. I will also protect anyone who keeps this Sutra so that he may have no troubles up to a distance of one hundred yojanas from here" (p. 327). Then he uttered more dharani-spells, vowing to protect any teacher of the Dharma.

Other supernatural members of the congregation did the same. They were a heavenly-king named World-Holder (Dhrtarasrta), ten raksasis (female demons), Hariti (their mother), and their attendants. All swore to protect teachers and keepers of the Sutra:

> We will never forgive anyone who troubles an expounder of the Lotus Sutra, even in a dream. Anyone who does not heed our spells but troubles an expounder of the law shall have his head split into seven pieces, just as the branches of an arjaka tree are split (pp. 328-9).

They went on to say how heavy would be the sin of anyone who dared to trouble an expounder of the Lotus Sutra (p. 329).

We should say a little more about dharanis. Bodhisattvas, who are practitioners of the Great Vehicle, are expected to practice and obtain the power of dharanis. In Chapter One, "Introduction," it says that there were eighty

thousand Bodhisattvas in the congregation, and all of them
"had obtained dharanis" (p. 1).

It is believed that the root of the word dharani in Sanskrit is the verb *dhuti,* which means "to keep or maintain."
Probably the original meaning of dharani was to keep or
maintain something in the memory. It was necessary for
people learning a sutra to be able to remember its words and
recite them accurately.

As the Sutra has said, there are five kinds of practice: to
keep, read, recite, expound, and copy the Sutra. To read,
which is the second of the five, means to read it by looking at
it. To recite, the third practice, means to know it by heart and
be able to read it without looking at it. Whenever you read
the Sutra, it is important to hold the sutra book in your hands
and read each word respectfully. It is not really necessary to
memorize it or be able to read it fast. However, from a practical point of view, it is helpful to be able to recite portions by
heart. Bodhisattvas, all of whom are also teachers, memorize
the words in order to teach them correctly. The power of
knowing the words by heart, a power which is common to
Bodhisattvas, is called the power of dharanis.

In a book called *Maha-prajna-paramitopadesa,* the
great Indian philosopher Nagarjuna (second century) says
about dharanis, "If a Bodhisattva obtains the power of
dharanis, he will never lose the Dharma from his memory,
but will keep it forever."

This idea was later developed to mean that if someone
continues in this practice diligently until he can recite an entire sutra by heart, he will obtain the miraculous power inher-
ent in that sutra. Phrases and words of the sutra are then
called dharani-spells. In the Lotus Sutra, the dharani-spells are
uttered to protect the practitioners, teachers, and expounders
of the Sutra.

The Sutra of the Lotus Flower of the Wonderful Law

CHAPTER XXVII: KING WONDERFUL-ADORNMENT
AS THE PREVIOUS LIFE OF A BODHISATTVA

(The Second Assembly on Mt. Sacred Eagle)

This chapter recounts how long, long ago, in the days of
Cloud-Thunderpeal-Star-King-Flower-Wisdom Buddha, there
lived a king named Wonderful-Adornment (Subhavyuha). He
had two children, Pure-Store (Vimalagarbha) and Pure-Eyes
(Vimalanetra), who were actually Medicine-King Bodhisattva
and Superior-Medicine Bodhisattva in previous lives. Their
father, Wonderful-Adornment, was, in a previous existence,
Flower-Virtue Bodhisattva (Padmasri). In this chapter, the
Buddha discusses the motivations and activities of these
Bodhisattvas in their former existences.

For long ages Pure-Store and Pure-Eyes had been practicing the way which Bodhisattvas should practice. They had
also practiced the Six Perfections, the thirty-seven ways to enlightenment, and various samadhis. At this time, Cloud-
Thunderpeal-Star-King-Flower-Wisdom Buddha wanted to
expound the Lotus Sutra to the king and his people. The two
sons went to their mother, Pure-Virtue (Vimaladatta), and said
to her, "Mother, please accompany us to pay homage to the
Buddha. He is about to expound the Lotus Sutra."

But the mother answered, "You know your father does not
believe in Buddhism, and will not approve of us going. He is
devoted to the teachings of the Brahmans. Go and speak with
him first, and see if he will come with us to hear the teachings
of the Buddha. Tell him that although you were born in this

family of wrong views, you are deeply concerned about his
future welfare. Then perform some miracle before him. If he
sees a miracle, he will change his mind and allow us to go and
see the Buddha."

So the two princes went to their father and performed extraordinary feats before him. They soared up into the sky
seven times higher than the height of a tala-tree, and walked,
stood, sat, and reclined in mid-air. They spewed water and
flames from different parts of their bodies. They swelled up
their bodies until they looked like giants; then they shrank
again. They walked on water and dove into the earth.

The father was so astonished by this magical display that
he pressed his palms together before them, asking, "How did
you learn to do such things? Who is your teacher?"

The sons answered, "O King, our teacher is Cloud-
Thunderpeal-Star-King-Flower-Wisdom Buddha, who is now
seated under the Bodhi-tree of seven treasures, preaching the
Lotus Sutra. He is our teacher; we are his disciples." Then the
father said, "I would like to see this man, myself. I will accompany you."

The two sons descended from the sky, went and reported
to their mother. "We have performed the Buddha's work for
our father's sake, and his eyes have been opened. Now please
allow us to renounce the world and practice the Way under
the Buddha." She gave them her permission. Then the two
sons said to their parents, "Go to Cloud-Thunderpeal-Star-
King-Flower-Wisdom Buddha and make offerings to him, because the chance to meet a Buddha is rare. It is as rare as
seeing the udumbara-flower open; it opens only once every
three thousand years. Or it is as rare as for a one-eyed sea-
turtle to come up through a hole in a piece of wood floating in
the vast ocean. We are all extremely fortunate to meet the
teaching of the Buddha in this very life. Permit us to renounce
the world and become his disciples" (p. 331-2).

Eighty-four thousand women in the palace of King Wonderful-Adornment also came to believe and accept the Lotus

Sutra. Pure-Eyes acquired the samadhi of the Lotus Flower of the Wonderful Law, and Pure-Store acquired the samadhi for the release from evil regions. Queen Pure-Virtue learned the samadhi for the assembly of the Buddhas, and understood the treasury of their hidden core.

In this way, King Wonderful-Adornment with his attendants, and their two sons with theirs all went before the Buddha, pressed their palms together in prayer, kneeled at his feet, and then withdrew to one side.

The Buddha expounded the Dharma for the King, and the King was so overcome with joy that he and the Queen removed the pearl necklaces from around their necks, and scattered their jewels about the Buddha. The necklaces changed into a jeweled platform with four pillars. As the Buddha sat upon the platform, he emitted a great, bright light from his body. Then, facing the audience, he said, "King Wonderful-Adornment, you will attain Buddhahood in the future, becoming a Buddha called Sala-tree King (Salaraja) in a world to be called Great-Light" (p. 332-3).

Hearing this, the King abdicated the throne to his younger brother, and he and his wife, their two sons, and all their attendants renounced the world; they practiced the teachings of the Lotus Sutra for eighty-four thousand years. After that, he practiced the samadhi for the adornment of all pure merits. He went up into the air seven times the height of a tala-tree, and said to the Buddha, "By the miracles they performed, these two sons of mine led me from wrong views to belief in the Lotus Sutra, and caused me to see you. My two sons are my teachers. I believe that they were reborn into my family as my virtuous sons for my benefit."

The Buddha praised him. "Yes, it is true, just as you say. Your two sons are praiseworthy teachers."

The king came down from the sky to the earth, pressed his palms together in prayer, and bowed. "Never again," he said, "will I believe in wrong teachings." After making this firm decision, he departed (p. 334).

This is an outline of the chapter. Here Sakyamuni clarifies the virtuous practice of Medicine-King Bodhisattva, who was one of the sons, and Superior-Medicine Bodhisattva, who was the other.

The Sutra of the Lotus Flower of the Wonderful Law

CHAPTER XXVIII: THE ENCOURAGEMENT OF UNIVERSAL-SAGE BODHISATTVA

(The Second Assembly on Mt. Sacred Eagle)

The meaning of this chapter's title is that Universal-Sage Bodhisattva (Samantabhadra) will appear before, protect, and encourage anyone who keeps and practices the Lotus Sutra, and he will have that person aspire to the Way to Buddhahood.

After the story of King Wonderful-Adornment was finished, Samantabhadra Bodhisattva, accompanied by many of his disciples, came from a world far away to the east of this World of Endurance. This Bodhisattva was famous for his virtues and supernatural powers. People in the lands he passed through welcomed him with showers of flowers and heavenly music. When he reached Mount Sacred Eagle, Samantabhadra bowed before Sakyamuni and said to him, "I have come from the country of Treasure-Power-Virtue-Superior-King Buddha in order to hear the Lotus Sutra. Please expound it for me and tell me how the good men and women who live after your extinction will be able to obtain it" (p. 336).

In answer to his question, Sakyamuni replied, "The good men and women will be able to obtain this sutra after my extinction if they do four things: (1) secure the protection of the Buddhas, (2) plant roots of virtue, (3) join with others who are firm in their resolution to seek enlightenment, and (4) resolve to save all living beings" (p. 336-7).

"World-Honored One," said Universal-Sage, "if people keep this Sutra in the defiled world in the later five hundred years after your extinction, I will protect them and free them from any troubles, so that they may live peacefully and not be exploited for their weak points. No demons will be able to exploit their weaknesses.

"If anyone reads and recites the Lotus Sutra while walking or standing, I will mount a kingly white elephant with six tusks, go to him with other great Bodhisattvas, show myself to him, make offerings to him, and protect him. If anyone sits and meditates upon this Sutra, I will mount the kingly white elephant and appear before him, too. If he forgets a phrase of a verse of the Sutra, I will remind him of it, and read and recite it with him so that he may understand it.

"If anyone wants to study and practice this Sutra, he or she should concentrate the mind strenuously for three weeks. At the end of the three weeks, I will mount the white elephant, make my presence known, expound the law, and cause that person to rejoice. I will also give him dharani-spells. Anyone who obtains these dharanis will never be killed by any nonhuman power nor be annoyed by worldly desires" (p. 337-8).

Samantabhadra uttered dharani-spells in front of the Buddha, and then said, "They should understand that it is only by my supernatural powers that a Bodhisattva can hear these dharanis. Anyone who keeps, reads, and recites the Lotus Sutra and practices it correctly is considered to be performing the practice of Universal-Sage. I will protect this Sutra with my supernatural powers so that it may be propagated in the world and never be destroyed" (p. 338-9).

Then Sakyamuni praised Universal-Sage. "Excellent, excellent, Universal-Sage! You will protect this Sutra so that many living beings may obtain peace and benefits. You, Universal-Sage, have already obtained inconceivable merits and great compassion. Anyone who keeps, reads, recites, and copies the Lotus Sutra should be considered to see me and hear this Sutra from my mouth. That person will be upright, and will not be troubled by the three poisons of greed, anger, and ignorance or other worldly desires. That person should be considered to be praised by me, to be caressed by me on the head, and to be covered with my robe.

"Universal-Sage! If you see anyone who keeps, reads, and recites this Sutra in the later five hundred years after my extinction, you should think, 'Before long, that person will go to the place of enlightenment, defeat the forces of evil, attain supreme enlightenment, expound the law to people far and near, and sit on the seat of the Dharma in the midst of a great multitude.'

"Whatever that person wishes for will not go unfulfilled. He or she will receive meritorious rewards even in this present life. On the other hand, those who abuse or insult an expounder of the Lotus Sutra will surely receive severe retribution. Therefore, Universal-Sage, whenever you see in the distance someone who is keeping this Sutra, you should rise from your seat, go to that person, and pay homage to him or her just as you pay homage to me" (p. 339-341).

This is the last chapter of the Lotus Sutra. By the merits of this teaching, as many Bodhisattvas as there are sands in the River Ganges obtained the dharanis of Samantabhadra Bodhisattva, and as many Bodhisattvas as the particles of dust filling the great universe grasped how to practice the Way of Universal-Sage.

When the Buddha finished expounding this Sutra, all the congregation, including Bodhisattvas, deities, and other living beings, rejoiced greatly, memorized the words of the Buddha, bowed before him, and departed from Mount Sacred Eagle.

THE SUTRA OF MEDITATION ON
UNIVERSAL-SAGE BODHISATTVA

Our discussion of the twenty-eight chapters of the Lotus Sutra has finished. The final section will be about the Sutra of Meditation on Universal-Sage Bodhisattva, which concludes the Threefold Lotus Sutra.

The name of this sutra is generally abbreviated as "the Universal-Sage Sutra," or "the Sutra of Repentance." [The name Universal-Sage, Samantabhadra, might also be translated as "Universal-Virtue" or "Universal-Good."]

After he had finished presenting the Lotus Sutra, Sakyamuni moved from Mount Sacred Eagle (Mt. Grdhrakuta, which means "Vulture Peak" in Sanskrit) to the country of Vaisali on the way to Kusinagara, where he would later enter Parinirvana (complete extinction). At the auditorium of the Great-Forest-Monastery in Vaisali, the Buddha told his followers that he would enter Nirvana in three more months. It is recorded that he was accompanied at that time by Ananda, the older Kasyapa brother, and Maitreya Bodhisattva. These three open the Universal Sutra by putting a question to the Buddha.

World-Honored One! After the extinction of the Buddha, how can living beings raise the mind of the Bodhisattva, practice the Mahayana sutras of the Great Vehicle, and rightly ponder the world of one reality? How can they keep from losing the aspiration for supreme Buddhahood? How, without cutting off their earthly cares and renouncing their five desires, can they also purify their sense organs and destroy their sins? How, with the natural pure eyes given by their parents and without forsaking their five desires, can they see things with all impediments?

The Buddha answered them.

Listen to me attentively, ponder, and remember what I say. On Mount Sacred Eagle and other places, the Buddha explained in detail the way of one reality. Now in this place, I will explain the Dharma to the living beings here present and others yet to be born, those who want to practice the supreme Dharma of the Great Vehicle and practice the works of Universal-Sage. I will now make clear to you the matter of eliminating numerous sins by anyone, whether he is able to see Universal-Sage or is unable to see him.

Ananda, if there are any among all living beings who recite the Great Vehicle, practice it, aspire to it, delight to see the form and body of Universal-Sage, take pleasure in seeing the stupa of Many-Treasures Buddha, take joy in seeking Sakyamuni Buddha and the manifestations of the Buddha emanated from him, and rejoice to obtain the purity of the six sense organs, they must learn this meditation. The merits of this meditation will free them from all hindrances and enable them to see the excellent forms. Even though they have not yet entered into samadhi, just by reciting and keeping the Great Vehicle, they will devote themselves to practicing it, and after having kept their minds continuously on the Great Vehicle for [as little as] a day or [as much as] three weeks, they will be able to see Universal-Sage Bodhisattva; those who have heavy impediments will see him after seven weeks; again, those who have an even heavier one will see him after one birth, two births, or three births.

Samantabhadra, Universal-Sage, is boundless in the size of his body, in the sound of his voice, and the form of his image. Desiring to come to this world, he makes use of his free transcendent powers and shrinks his stature to the small size of a human being. Because the people in Jambudvipa ["greater

India," the inhabited world] have the three heavy hindrances [of arrogance, envy, and greed], by his wisdom power he appears transformed as mounted on a white elephant. The elephant has six tusks and supports its body on seven legs.

According to the sutra, the elephant has six tusks and supports itself on seven legs. This symbolic description is said to mean six pure sense organs and seven qualities of wisdom, which are mindfulness, investigation of the law, energy, rapture, repose, concentration (samadhi), and equanimity. Universal-Sage himself is described next.

There is a Bodhisattva who sits cross-legged [on the elephant]. His body, pure as a white jewel, radiates fifty rays of fifty different colors, forming a brightness around his head. From the pores of his body he emits rays of light, and innumerable emanated Buddhas are at the ends of the rays, accompanied by retinues of emanated Bodhisattvas.

Sakyamuni then explains how to visualize Universal-Sage:

At first, the practitioner must make a vow to see Universal-Sage Bodhisattva and must worship all the Buddhas and Bodhisattvas in the ten directions. He or she must then practice the Dharma of Repentance, read and recite sutras of the Great Vehicle, make offerings to people who uphold the Great Vehicle, and regard all people with compassion just as the Buddha does.

If a person reflects like this, Universal-Sage Bodhisattva will emit a golden light from his whole body, and the light will illuminate innumerable worlds in the east and make the whole universe shine with the color of gold. The practitioner will see it and feel full of joy in both mind and body.

Furthermore, the practitioner will believe correctly in the teaching of Samantabhadra, consider it correctly, and gradually will be able to inwardly see that the body of the Buddha

in the east is golden colored, beautiful, majestic, and wonderful. Once the practitioner has seen one Buddha, he or she will see another and another. Gradually the practitioner will make out all the Buddhas in the east, and then all the Buddhas in the ten directions.

Having seen the Buddhas, the practitioner will feel joyful, and say, "By means of the Great Vehicle, I have been able to see all the Bodhisattvas, and by means of their powers, I have been able to see all the Buddhas. Although I have seen those Buddhas, I am still unable to see them clearly. If I close my eyes, I can see them; but if I open my eyes, I lose sight of them."

After saying this, the practitioner universally makes obeisance, prostrating down to the ground towards the Buddhas in the ten directions. After doing this, he or she should kneel with folded hands, and say, "The Buddhas, the World-Honored Ones, possess the ten powers, fearlessness, the eighteen unique characteristics, the great mercy, the great compassion, and the three kinds of stability in contemplation. These Buddhas, forever remaining in this world, have the finest appearance of all forms. Because of what sin [that I have committed] am I unable to see them [with my eyes, and not just mentally]?"

After speaking in this way, the practitioner should repent still more. Once he has achieved pure repentance, Samantabhadra will again appear before him, and will not leave his side, whether he is walking, standing, sitting, or lying down, and even in dreams will teach him the Dharma. After awakening from these dreams, the practitioner will take delight in the law. After twenty-one days and nights have passed in this way, the practitioner will acquire the Dharani of the Void.

Then the practitioner will rejoice still more, and universally salute the Buddhas in all directions. After he has saluted the Buddhas in all directions, Samantabhadra, who is now abiding always before him, will teach him and explain all his karmic debts and the environments of his former lives, urging him to confess all his [accumulated] sins.

Once he has confessed all his sins, the practitioner will attain the Samadhi of the Void. Having attained this samadhi, he will clearly see the Buddha Aksobhya ("Immovable") in the east and the Pure Land of Wonderful Joy.

If the practitioner practices the Dharma of Repentance for a day or twenty-one days, he or she will obtain the Samadhi of the Revelation of the Buddhas to All Men, the purity of the six sense organs, and be able to see the figures of countless Buddhas. The Buddhas will tell him, "You are a practitioner of the Great Vehicle, an aspirant to the spirit of Great-Adornment, and one who keeps the Great Vehicle in mind. When we first aspired to Buddhahood, we were just like you. Because we practiced [the Great Vehicle] in our former lives, we have now become pure bodies of the All Wise. . . ."

These Great Vehicle sutras are the Dharma-treasury of the Buddhas, the eyes of the Buddhas from all directions in the past, present, and future, and also the seed which produces the Tathagatas of the past, present, and future. The practitioner who upholds these sutras has the body of a Buddha and does the work of a Buddha. Know that such a one is an apostle sent by the Buddhas; this person is covered by the robes of the Buddhas; he or she is a true Dharma-heir of the Buddhas. You should practice the Great Vehicle and not cut off the Dharma seeds.

Sakyamuni continues by teaching what the Buddha's pure lands look like, how the practitioner can see the Buddhas there one after the other, and how important it is for one who wishes to see the Buddhas to read and recite the sutras of the Great Vehicle.

The [Buddha-]lands are even, with no knolls, hills, or briars, but with grounds of lapis lazuli and roadways lined with golden strands. . . . [Then the practitioner will see] a jewel tree which always produces deep gold and white silver, and is adorned with the seven treasures. Under this tree there is a jeweled lion-throne; the lion throne is two thousand yojanas high, and from the throne radiates the light of a hundred jewels. In the same manner, from all the trees, the other jewel-thrones, and each jewel-throne there radiates the light of a hundred jewels. In the same manner, from all the trees, the other jewel-thrones, and from each jewel-throne emerge five hundred white elephants on which are seated all the Bodhisattvas emanated from Universal-Sage. Thereupon the practitioner, making obeisance to all the emanations of Universal-Sage, should say, 'By what sin [that I have committed in the past] have I been able to see only the jewel-grounds, jewel-thrones, and jewel-trees, but not the Buddhas themselves?'

When the practitioner has said this, he or she will see that on each of the jewel thrones sits a World-Honored One, magnificent in his majesty. Having now seen the Buddhas, the practitioner will be delighted, and will continue to study and recite the Great Vehicle sutras. By the power of the Great Vehicle, a voice will come from the sky, saying, "Because of the merit you have acquired by practicing the Great Vehicle, you have seen the Buddhas. However, you have not yet been able to see Sakyamuni Buddha, the duplicate Buddhas emanated from him, and the stupa of Many-Treasures."

[Being thus reminded by the voice in the sky], the practitioner will be even more zealous in reciting and studying the Great Vehicle sutras. Because he studies the "Sutras of Great Extent," the Great Vehicle, even in his dreams he will see Sakyamuni Buddha preaching the Law-Flower Sutra to the great congregation on Mount Sacred Eagle, and expounding the meaning of the One Vehicle.

After hearing and seeing this [in dreams], the practitioner will yearn to hear and see the Buddha [even while awake]. Folding his hands together in supplication, and kneeling in the direction of Mount Sacred Eagle, he will say, "Tathagata, [I know] the World's Hero remains in this world forever. Out of compassion for me, please reveal yourself to me!"

Then he will see Mount Sacred Eagle adorned with the seven treasures and filled with countless monks, "hearers," and a great multitude. This place is lined with jewel-trees, and

its jeweled ground is smooth and even. Seated there [in ethe-
real glory] is Sakyamuni. He sends forth from between his
eyebrows a ray of light, which illuminates the ten quarters of
the universe, passing through innumerable worlds in all directions. Wherever this ray of light reaches, the Buddhas emanated from Sakyamuni Buddha assemble like a great cloud,
and preach the wonderful law, just as it says in the Sutra of the
Lotus Flower of the Wonderful Law. Each of these emanated
Buddhas has a body the color of deep gold, is boundless in
size, and sits upon a lion-throne. Each of them is accompanied by a retinue of hundreds of kotis of great Bodhisattvas."

These lines explain that when a practitioner wants to see
the Buddha, and by the merit of reading and reciting the
Mahayana sutras, he or she can visualize the Buddha by the
following steps: (1) At first, the practitioner will be able to see
Samantabhadra (Universal-Sage) Bodhisattva; (2) then the
practitioner will be able to see the Buddhas, the World-
honored Ones, but not Sakyamuni Buddha, his emanated
Buddhas, or the stupa of Many-Treasures; (3) if the practitioner continues to read and recite the Great Vehicle sutras, he
or she will be able to see them while dreaming; (4) finally, if
the practitioner continues studying and reciting the sutras, he
or she will see them while awake. In other words, the more
practitioners read and recite the Great Vehicle sutras, the
more clearly they can see the figures of the Buddhas.

The next part of this sutra deals with the teaching of
repentance of the six sense organs, the eyes, ears, nose,
tongue, body and mind. This section makes up the greater
part of the Meditation Sutra.

The goal of the repentance of the six sense organs is to
correctly purify the desires and karmas which our minds and
bodies have inherited [from past lives] and are causing attachments to be formed in our minds and bodies [today]. In Buddhism, it is taught that if we can purify our six sense organs,
we human beings will be able to enjoy a pure mind in a pure
body. Let us now look at these repentances one by one:

The Organ of the Eye

Universal-Sage Bodhisattva enters the heart of the practitioner, saying, "In your innumerable former lives, by reason of your organ of the eye, you have been attached to all forms. Because of your attachment to forms, you hanker after all dust. Because of your hankering after dust, you receive a woman's body and you are pleasurably absorbed in all forms everywhere that you are born for eon after eon. Forms harm your [inner] eyes and make you a slave to human desires. Therefore forms cause you to wander in the triple world. You become so accustomed to the triple world that you are blind to everything else . . . if you feel remorse for your sins, you will see Sakyamuni Buddha, the Buddhas emanated from him, and countless other Buddhas. You will not fall into evil paths for asamkhya kalpas. Thanks to the power and promise of the Great Vehicle, you will become an attendant of the Buddhas, just like all the Bodhisattvas who are reciting the dharanis."

The Organ of the Ear

Universal-Sage Bodhisattva says, "Throughout many eons, as a result of your organ of hearing, you have been controlled by the voices of the external world. Your very hearing of beautiful sounds begets attachment to them. Your hearing of evil sounds causes the harm of one hundred and eight illusions. Retribution of your evil hearing brings about evil things, and your incessant hearing of evil sounds produces various entanglements. Because of your evil hearing sense, you fall into wrong paths, and are taken to faraway places, where the Dharma is unknown. Now, however, you are reciting and keeping the Great Vehicle, which is the oceanic store of merits. For this reason, you can see the Buddhas in the ten directions, and the stupa of Many-Treasures Buddha emerges to bear witness to you."

The Organ of the Nose

Universal-Sage speaks: "In the innumerable eons of your former lives, because of your attachments to odors, your discrimination and perceptions are attached to all kinds of external conditions, and you fall into birth and death. You should now meditate on the cause of the Great Vehicle. The cause of the Great Vehicle is the Reality of All Existence."

The Organ of the Tongue

This time the practitioner hears, not Samantabhadra but a voice from the sky, which says, "the errors of the tongue are boundless and numberless. All the thrones of evil karmas come from the organ of the tongue. A [loose] tongue cuts off the wheel of the Righteous Law. It cuts off the seeds of merits. The preaching of meaningless things is frequently forced on others. Praising false views is like adding wood to a fire and further wounding living beings, who already are suffering in raging flames. The recompense for such sins is evil paths for hundreds of thousands of eons. Outright lying is even worse; it causes one to fall into hell."

The Organ of the Body and the Organ of the Mind

The voice from the sky says, "The sins of the body are killing, stealing, and committing adultery, while the sins of the mind consist of entertaining thoughts of such evils. They produce the ten evil karmas and five deadly sins: 1) killing one's mother; 2) killing one's father; 3) killing a saint; 4) wounding a Buddha; and 5) destroying the harmony of the Sangha. The karmas of these six sense organs, with their branches, twigs, flowers, and leaves, fill the triple world, the twenty-five abodes of living beings, and all places where living beings are born. These evil karmas also increase the sufferings of the twelve causes, such as ignorance, old age, and death. You should now repent of all the evil karmas you have ever made."

Hearing these things, the practitioners repent sincerely and purify their six sense organs of body and mind. This sutra tells us that practitioners should read and recite the Great Vehicle sutras in order to purify their six sense organs, and by its merits and rewards, they can repent [properly], purify their six sense organs, and see Sakyamuni Buddha, his emanated duplicates, and the stupa of Many-Treasures. Sakyamuni then summarizes the teaching of repentance in verses.

If you have evil in your eye-organ,
And your eyes are impure with karmic impediments,
You should recite the Great Vehicle sutras,
And reflect on the repentance of the eye,
Ending all visual karmas forever.

Your ear-organ hears disordered sounds,
Disturbing the principle of harmony.
This produces a demented mind within you.
Just recite the Great Vehicle sutras,
And meditate on the void non-aspect of the Truth,
Ending all longstanding evils,
So that with celestial ears
You may hear sounds from all directions.

The organ of smell is attached to certain odors,
Causing contacts according to preferences.
If you recite the Great Vehicle sutras,
And meditate on the fundamental truth of the Dharma,
You will become free of evil karmas,
And not produce them again in future lives.

By evil speech, the tongue-organ
Causes five kinds of evil karmas.

If you wish to bring them under control,
Practice only deeds of mercy,
And thinking on the true principle
Of quiescence of the Dharma,
Get rid of feelings of discrimination!

The mind never rests,
But is like a monkey
[jumping from branch to branch].
If you wish to quiet this organ,
You must zealously recite the Great Vehicle sutras,
Reflect on the Buddha's greatly enlightened body,
The completion of his power,
And his fearlessness.

The body directs its organs,
As wind causes dust to roll about.
If you wish to destroy these evils,
Remove ancient dusty illusions,
Dwell peacefully in the castle of Nirvana,
And be at ease with a tranquil mind,
You must recite the Great Vehicle sutras,
And meditate on the Mother of Bodhisattvas . . .

The Ocean of Impediment of all karmas
Is caused by your false imagination.
Sit upright and meditate on the true aspect of reality!
All sins are just like [morning] frost and dew;
The [rising] sun of wisdom will dissolve them.

Therefore with complete devotion,
Repent of your six sense organs!

"The impediment of all karmas" is as vast as an ocean. However, it was all produced by the illusions of living beings. This sutra tells us that, in order to remove all bad karmas, we should repent. To repent does not mean just to apologize for making mistakes. It means to actually remove all self-attachment from our mind, and give full play to the Buddha-nature which has existed within us from the beginning. It also means to practice the Great Vehicle and cultivate our Buddha-wisdom. Therefore, the sutra says that we must be upright, and in meditation consider the true aspect of reality.

The sins of human beings are just like frost and dew. When they are warmed by the sun, they melt away naturally. Likewise, this sutra says that if we cultivate Buddha-wisdom, many sins will disappear by themselves. To cultivate the Buddha-wisdom from the bottom of our hearts is the real meaning of repentance. Sakyamuni explains further:

> I, the Bodhisattvas in this auspicious eon, and all the Buddhas in the ten directions, have now rid ourselves of the sins of birth and death [accumulated] during hundreds of myriads of kotis of asamkhya kalpas, by realizing the true meaning of the Great Vehicle. By means of this supreme and wonderful law of repentance, we have become Buddhas in the ten directions. If you wish to accomplish perfect enlightenment quickly, and wish in your present life to see the Buddhas in all directions as well as the Bodhisattva Universal-Sage, you must dwell in a secluded place, bathe and purify yourself, put on clean robes, burn rare incense, recite and read the Great Vehicle sutras, and think on the meaning of the Great Vehicle.
>
> If there are any living beings who salute the Buddhas in ten directions six times a day and night, recite the Great Vehicle sutras, and consider the profound truth of the void, they will rid themselves of the sins of birth and death produced during hundreds of myriads of kotis of asamkhya kalpas in the short time it takes to snap one's fingers. Those who are doing this work are the real children of the Buddha. The Buddhas in all directions and the Bodhisattvas will become their preceptors. Such people are called perfect in the precepts of the Bodhisattvas. . . .
>
> If a practitioner wishes to receive the precepts of the Bodhisattvas, he or she should be in a quiet place, worship

the Buddhas in the ten directions, repent his sins, and say, "Sakyamuni Buddha, the World-Honored One! Manjusri, possessor of great compassion! Maitreya Bodhisattva, supreme and greatly merciful sun! All Buddhas in the ten directions! Great Bodhisattvas! The Three Treasures! I devote myself to all of you. May Sakyamuni Buddha be my preceptor, and may Manjusri Bodhisattva be my teacher!"

PRAYER

Having said this, the practitioner should burn rare incense as offering, scatter flowers, and affirm, "I have now raised the aspiration for Buddhahood; may this merit save all living beings!"

Whether one is a monk or a nun or a lay person, he or she has no need of preceptor, nor the need to employ any teacher; even without attending the ceremony of Jnapti-karman [monastic confession prior to ordination], because of the power coming from receiving and keeping, reading and reciting the Great Vehicle sutras, and because of the works which Universal-Sage Bodhisattva helps and inspires him to do, such a practitioner is the eyes of the Righteous Law of all the Buddhas in the ten directions. One will be able, through this Dharma, to perform by oneself the five kinds of Dharma-bodies (precepts, meditation, wisdom, emancipation, and knowledge of emancipation). This Law will be the assurance of attaining Buddhahood.

Suppose that Sravakas infringe many precepts and the rules of proper behavior because of their ignorance or evil minds. If they wish to rid themselves of these sins and destroy these errors, they should diligently read the Great Vehicle sutras, consider the profound fundamental principle of the Void, and bring his wisdom of the Void into their hearts. Know that in each one of their thoughts they will gradually end the defilement of their longstanding sins, and purify themselves.

Suppose laymen do evil deeds, seek greedily and untiringly after base desires, commit the five deadly sins, slander the sutras of Great Extent, and perform the ten evil karmas. Recompense for such great evils will cause them to fall into evil paths, and they will be sure to sink down to the great hell *Avichi*. If they wish to rid themselves of and destroy these impediments of karmas, they should raise shame and repent all their sins.

What is the law of repentance for lay people? The law of repentance for lay people is to constantly have the right mind, not slander the Three Treasures, not hinder monks, and not persecute anyone practicing brahma-conduct. They should not forget to practice the law of the six reflections [on the Buddha, the Law, the Brotherhood, moral precepts, alms-giving, and the Pure Land]; they should greet, respect, and support any keeper of the Great Vehicle.

There are five laws of repentance. The first is to think of the profound doctrines of the sutras and the first principle of the Void. The second is to discharge their filial duties to their parents, and to respect their teachers and elders. The third to supervise, within their spheres of influence, by means of the Righteous Dharma, and not unjustly oppress their subordinates. The fourth is to issue within their spheres of influence an ordinance for six days of fasting every month (the 8th, 14th, 15th, 23rd, 29th, and 30th days), the days when people are to abstain from killing any living thing. The fifth is to believe deeply the causes and results of things, to have faith in the way of One Reality, and to know that the Buddha is never extinct. . . .

If in the future, there be any who practice these laws of repentance, know that such a person will attain perfect enlightenment before long.

The Lotus Sutra tells us in its last chapter, "Encouragement of Universal-Sage Bodhisattva," that if someone upholds, reads, recites, and practices correctly, Universal-Sage will surely reveal himself to that person and protect him or her. That person will attain supreme-perfect-enlightenment and be led to the attainment of Buddhahood. On the other hand, anyone who criticizes or slanders a practitioner of the Lotus Sutra will receive evil recompense.

Basing itself on this teaching of the Lotus Sutra, the Sutra of Meditation on Universal-Sage Bodhisattva teaches us practical techniques to put the Dharma into effect, particularly by undertaking the law of repentance and visualizing the figure of Universal-Sage, and the importance of reading and reciting the Lotus Sutra, which is the epitome of all the sutras of the Great Vehicle.

Appendix

THE LOTUS SUTRA AND NICHIREN

The best known version of the Lotus Sutra is the Chinese translation made in Changan, then the capital of China, by Kumarajiva in 406. More than fifteen centuries have passed since then. After Kumarajiva's lucid translation had appeared the Lotus Sutra was studied and analyzed by such scholars as Tao-sheng (d. 434), Fa-yun (467-529), and Chi-tsang (549-623). However, it was Great Master Chih-i (538-597) who integrated their studies and established the basic theory of the Lotus Sutra.

The theory of Chih-i was introduced into Japan by Saicho (767-822; his posthumous name was Dengyo Daishi), and his students and spiritual heirs continued to study the Sutra. Ever since its introduction into Japan, the Lotus Sutra has attracted not only academic enthusiasts but also a broad popular following. These centuries of academic studies as well as popular faith in the Sutra were eventually synthesized by Nichiren (1222-1282).

The studies conducted over so many centuries made possible a deeper understanding of the Lotus Sutra, and methodological standards for its interpretation were established. One example is called *Kamon*. It is a classification of the twenty-eight chapters into several sets for a systematic explanation of their meaning.

The major *Kamon* is the "Three Parts of Each of the Two Divisions of the Lotus Sutra" which was established by Great Master Chih-i. Most commentators since his time have accepted his guidelines.

As we mentioned before, the "Three Parts of Each of the Two Divisions of the Lotus Sutra" refers to the division of the Sutra into two main sections: the first half, consisting of Chapters One through Fourteen, and the second half, consisting of Chapters Fifteen through Twenty-eight. *Kamon* gives a detailed explanation of the reason for this division. The first half is named *Shakumon*, literally "imprinted gate." Its main purpose is to teach how "hearers" and Pratyekabuddhas can attain Buddhahood in the One Vehicle. The second half is called Hommon, which means "Primal Gate" or "Primal Mystery." This part reveals Sakyamuni to be the infinite, absolute Buddha, the Buddha who attained enlightenment in the remotest past but still leads living beings in the present. These two points are considered the fundamental ideas of the Lotus Sutra.

The division of a text into three parts is common to nearly all sutras, not just the Lotus Sutra. The first part, Introductory, tells mainly when and where the sutra was taught, and by whom. The second part is the core teaching of that particular sutra. The third and final part, called the Conclusion or Propagation, tells how the sutra was received by its audience, and how it should be kept and transmitted to future generations. However, we can see some marked differences between the Lotus Sutra and other scriptures when we compare them according to this threefold structure.

First of all, in most sutras, the Introductory and Propagation parts are short and sweet, serving merely structural functions to complete the whole. In contrast, the Lotus Sutra contains a detailed introduction in addition to a general preface. This detailed introduction, unique to the Lotus Sutra, presents teachings that foreshadow what will be expounded in the following chapters. Secondly, the Lotus Sutra is structured as if the conclusion incorporates the main part. For example, after Chapter Ten, "The Teacher of the Dharma," most chapters in the second division deal with the matter of keeping and propagating the Sutra in future worlds, which is, in fact, the major characteristic of a conclusion. Apparently Chih-i made his structural division based on this idea. Here is a summary of his *Kamon:*

Three Parts of Each of the Two Divisions

I. *Shakumon*
The Realm of Trace or Imprinted Gate (Chapter One, "Introductory," to Chapter Fourteen, "Peaceful Practices.")

    1. *Introduction:* Chapter One.
    2. *The Main Part:* Chapter Two, "Expedients," to Chapter Nine, "The Assurance of Future Buddhahood of the Sravakas Who Have Something More to Learn and of the Sravakas Who Have Nothing More to Learn."
    3. *Conclusion:* Chapter Ten, "The Teacher of the Dharma," to Chapter Fourteen, "Peaceful Practices."

II. *Hommon*
The Realm of Origin or Primal Mystery.

    1. *Introduction:* The first half of Chapter Fifteen, "The Appearance of Bodhisattvas from Underground."
    2. *The Main Part:* The second half of Chapter Fifteen to the first half of Chapter Seventeen, "The Variety of Merits," with Chapter Sixteen as its core. This is called the "one chapter and two halves."
    3. *Conclusion:* From the second half of Chapter Seventeen to Chapter Twenty-eight, "Encouragement of Universal-Sage Bodhisattva."

This clear-cut classification indicates that the Lotus Sutra was formed in such a way that its principal ideas unfold gradually as the chapters proceed. It would be interesting to go deeper into the philosophical reasoning behind this classification, but we will have to be content here with an outline of the major teachings of the text.

The Unification of Doctrine

The first half of the Lotus Sutra (*Shakumon*) expounds the teaching of the One Vehicle. The several schools of Buddhism, which are divided roughly into three types (Sravaka-Vehicle, Pratyekabuddha-Vehicle, and Bodhisattva-Vehicle), are unified in the one single teaching of the One Vehicle. Since the number three represents all the various Buddhist Teachings, "three" here implies "many" or "all."

The Dharma which was attained and taught by Sakyamuni is the Universal Truth or Law, which must be acknowledged by every human being. There is only one Truth. However, so that people could understand it better, Sakyamuni expounded the one Truth in various ways, according to the capacities of his listeners. The varieties in Sakyamuni's teaching show that the Truth is not rigid; rather it is flexible enough to be presented in different forms, according to the circumstances, despite its oneness. This is the reason Sakyamuni's numerous sutras can be said to compose one and the same teaching. Unfortunately, sectarians, who did not understand the unity of Truth, began to turn these partial truths against each other and vie with each other for superiority. Their teachings, diverse as they may appear, are still united in the single teaching of the Buddha. The concept of the unification of doctrines is the very core of the teaching of the One Vehicle.

The idea of the One Vehicle can be applied to the secular world as well. The diversification of world culture has created differences in ideas, or in the ways of thinking, among nations. Human culture has developed as a result of our search for the ultimate truth. In the process of cultural advancement through the pursuit of ultimate truth, conflicts often emerge due to our many theoretical differences. History tells us that these confrontations sometimes lead to bitter disputes or even war. Despite all differences in the process, however, these theories or ideas must eventually be unified, because they are all leading to the one single goal of the ultimate truth. The Lotus Sutra clarifies this concept through the teaching of the One Vehicle.

The Unification of Faith

In Buddhism, various Buddhas have been established as objects of devotion for different pious believers. Since each Buddha has a good reason for being venerated, Buddhism permits us to worship any or all of them. Nevertheless, the Most-Venerable-One should be One, just as the Truth is One. The second half of the Lotus Sutra (*Hommon*) emphasizes such a Buddhist position regarding unity of faith. As the object of faith is absolute, it must relate to the realm of eternity. Generally we think of Sakyamuni as a historical figure, bound by the limitations of time and space, and only a provisional manifestation of the infinite, eternal Buddha. According to the Lotus Sutra, however, every Buddha, including the historical Sakyamuni Buddha, is a representation of the eternal original being of Sakyamuni.

Sakyamuni, when seen as the eternal being, is called the Original Buddha (*Hombutsu*), who was enlightened in the remotest past. The other Buddhas are called "manifestations of the Buddha." The existence of each of them is a provisional manifestation in some time or place of the Original Buddha. The second half of the Lotus Sutra (*Hommon*) reveals the concept of the eternity of Sakyamuni, in contrast with the historical Buddha, who is a temporal representation of himself.

The idea of unity of doctrine, which we discussed above, should lead logically to the concept of unity of faith. Although the ultimate Truth is one in essence, human beings have various conflicting ideas about it. Nevertheless, we are able to advance toward a higher truth, overcoming conceptual conflicts, since we all believe firmly that the Truth is only one. Indeed, human progress is possible only because we are confident of the existence of a Universal Truth. After all, it is our confidence in the ultimate Truth that leads to the formation of our attitudes toward faith.

The Sutra's Philosophy of Life

Another outstanding characteristic of the Lotus Sutra is its practical teachings which can be adapted to our daily lives. The Buddhist faith often expounds difficult doctrines consisting of abstract philosophical ideas. When it comes to the Lotus Sutra, however, such complicated dogmas do not appear on the surface. For this reason, some critics have argued that there are no doctrines in the Lotus Sutra. But this is not true. The Lotus Sutra does contain profound philosophical thoughts. Instead of using tortuous logic, however, the Sutra explains its philosophy in the simplified form of stories, drawing on examples familiar to us from everyday life. This is why we find many parables in the text.

The Lotus Sutra contains seven parables, three of which are best known. The first is the "Parable of the Burning House of the Triple World" in Chapter Three. The second is the "Parable of the Rich Man and His Poor Son" in Chapter Four. The "Parable of the Physician and His Children" is presented in Chapter Sixteen. These three parables allegorically show the relationship between the Buddha and living beings by presenting a parental relationship. That is, faith in the Buddha is similar to the faith of a child in his father; and the Buddha's compassion toward living beings is like a father's love for his children. In other words, natural feelings drawn from the norms of everyday life eventually lead us toward faith in the Buddha.

In Chapter Nineteen, "Merits of a Teacher of the Dharma," we read, "When they expound the scriptures of non-Buddhist schools, or give advice to the government, or teach the way to earn a livelihood, they will be able to be in accord with the right teachings of the Buddha" (p. 282). This means that any study of secular issues, such as politics and economics, must be in accord with the cosmic law, which is to say, the Truth expounded in the Sutra. Conversely, the teachings of the Lotus Sutra (The Truth) are applicable to secular studies, such as politics or economics, whose prime objectives are the betterment of everyday life.

The Predictions for Future Ages After the Buddha's Extinction

Most teachers conclude their teachings with similar scenes, such as those in which Sakyamuni entrusts his disciples to propagate the sutra after his extinction. For this reason, the concluding part of a sutra is generally called the "Propagation."

In contrast, the Lotus Sutra contains many chapters which treat the matter of its propagation. According to the *Kamon* classification, there are seventeen chapters in all which discuss propagation: five chapters in the first half *(Shakumon)*, and twelve chapters in the second half *(Hommon)*. In other words, more than four-sevenths of all the chapters contain teachings concerning propagation of the Sutra. There is no other sutra which devotes so much attention to the matter of propagation. This is a feature unique to the Lotus Sutra. This fact alone tells us that the section of Propagation in this particular Sutra does not consist of just the concluding words. Rather, it is presented as an integral part of the way of Buddhist practice, a way which involves keeping and promoting the teachings of Sakyamuni in future centuries, long after his physical departure.

Of course, we today are not contemporaries of Sakyamuni, but live in an era after his extinction. In this sense, the Lotus Sutra can be seen as a sutra which was written particularly for us, who would live in the worlds after the Buddha's extinction. This point conveys a great significance which no other scriptures proclaim so clearly.

The Lotus Sutra and Nichiren

Throughout the long history of admiration for the Lotus Sutra, there were many readers and devotees who contributed to its propagation. But only Nichiren devoted his life to reading the Lotus Sutra to such a profound extent, putting both his body and soul into understanding it.

Nichiren suffered numerous religious persecutions which jeopardized even his life. Thanks to these ordeals, however, he gained a deeper understanding of the Lotus Sutra, through which he was able to enter the realm of Buddhist Truth.

The life-long experience of religious persecutions is unique to this saint, amounting to special ordeals worse than most ordinary men could endure. Nichiren himself was aware of this, which is why he said, "Nichiren alone is able to read the words of the Sutra."

The Lotus Sutra frequently maintains that it should be propagated far and wide and instructs the Bodhisattvas how to undertake this task. This particular section is commonly called the "Propagation" or "Conclusion." As we said, other sutras deal with this matter very briefly at the end of the book. In the Lotus Sutra, on the other hand, chapters discussing the matter of propagation account for four-sevenths of the total number. Indeed, the great emphasis on propagation is one of the most marked characteristics of the Lotus Sutra.

The Lotus Sutra can be seen as a book of prophetic teachings. For this reason, Nichiren called these teachings, "narratives of the Buddha in the future." These narratives of the future, however, do not merely prophesy what will happen in coming generations. Their point is that Sakyamuni teaches living beings how to perform practices in an era when he does not physically exist. Since the words of the Buddha are true, we are expected to accept them as the Truth, and we are all required to follow the teaching.

Nichiren actually put into practice what the Lotus Sutra had expounded concerning its propagation in the future. His determined efforts, however, raised opposition, which led to persecutions. Let us take a brief look at how the saint interpreted some of the words of the Sutra through his personal suffering.

On May 12, 1261, the Japanese military government arrested Nichiren, who was forty years old at the time. His arrest was followed by exile to Ito on the Izu Peninsula. During his exile, he wrote his essay, "Four Debts of Gratitude," in which he says:

> In the Age of Degeneration of the Buddha's teachings, anyone who believes so much as a word or a phrase of the Lotus Sutra is destined to be envied and hated. That is why the Lotus Sutra says, "Many people begrudge [the sutra] even in my lifetime. Needless to say, more people will do so after my extinction." When I [Nichiren] first read this phrase, I doubted it. But now my experience has convinced me that the Buddha's words are true. . . . Although I do not eat meat or fish, and have never harmed a living thing, and although I do not go about with a wife and child, I am treated as a criminal monk, just because I am propagating the teaching of the Lotus Sutra. . . . But when I realize that I am suffering persecutions by demons who have entered the bodies of my tormentors, just because I believe in the Lotus Sutra and follow its teachings, exactly as the Sutra expounds [in Chapter Thirteen, "Encouragement for Keeping the Sutra"], then I feel joy beyond words. I rejoice because I have found that even a man of low birth [such as I], one who is ignorant and uneducated, was forecast in the Lotus Sutra some two thousand years ago. The Buddha predicted that such a person [as I] "will suffer religious persecutions."

Here Nichiren expresses his pleasure at seeing his own experience vindicating the teachings of the Lotus Sutra. For example, Chapter Ten predicts, "If you expound the Sutra after the Buddha's extinction, many people will begrudge it," and Chapter Thirteen foretells, "Three kinds of devils will enter the bodies of monks and cause them to persecute the teachers of the Dharma." Such adversities actually befell Nichiren, as the words of the Sutra had foretold. So Nichiren accepted his misfortunes as living proofs of the words of the Sutra.

On September 12, 1271, when he was fifty years old, the government again arrested Nichiren. This time officials secretly attempted to behead him at Tatsu-no-Kuchi on the seashore near Kamakura. But a sudden miracle spared Nichiren and the government had to exile him instead to the Island of Sado. During his exile on Sado, the saint further deepened his religious contemplation and wrote some of his major works, such as *Kaimoku-sho* ("Opening the Eyes") and *Kanjin-honzon-sho* ("The Most-Venerable-One Revealed by Introspection"). In these writings, Nichiren clarified the practical significance of the Great Bodhisattvas from underground, including Superb-Action Bodhisattva, as the propagators of the Primal Mystery *(Hommon)* in the evil ages after the extinction of the Buddha.

As we have said, the Lotus Sutra can be divided into two sections: the first half *(Shakumon)* and the second half *(Hommon)*. Nichiren concluded that the fundamental idea of the Lotus Sutra is manifested more clearly in the latter half than the first half. Furthermore, the central idea of the second half is elaborated in Chapter Sixteen, "The Duration of the Life of the Buddha." The account in Chapter Sixteen is actually a continuation of the latter half of the previous chapter, "Bodhisattvas from Underground," and is continued through the first half of the next Chapter, "The Variety of Merits." The three parts are closely enough related to form one single chain of thought. In his *Kanjin-honzon-sho*, Nichiren argues that the quintessence of the teachings of the Primal Mystery lies in this chain of three parts, which he specifically calls the "one chapter and two halves." In addition, he declares that in our present Age of Degeneration, the teaching of the "one chapter and two halves" should be propagated in the abbreviated form of five Chinese characters, the title MYO-HO-REN-

GE-KYO, meaning "The Sutra of the Lotus Flower of the Wonderful Dharma."

His argument could be summarized as follows. In Chapter Fifteen of the Lotus Sutra, the ground was split open before Sakyamuni, and countless Bodhisattvas sprang up from underground, one after the other. Among these Bodhisattvas, who are commonly called the "Bodhisattvas from Underground," were four leaders: (1) Superb-Action (or Practice), (2) Limitless-Action, (3) Pure-Action, (4) Steadily-Established-Action. In Chapter Sixteen, Sakyamuni reveals his eternal nature, and further explains that the Bodhisattvas from Underground are in fact the disciples of this Eternal Buddha.

In Chapter Twenty-one, "Supernatural Powers of the Tathagatas," Sakyamuni authorizes these Great Bodhisattvas from Underground to propagate the Lotus Sutra after his extinction. Besides, the Buddha teaches that the heart of the Sutra's teachings should be manifested through four key dharmas: (1) all the teachings of the Tathagata, (2) all the unhindered, supernatural powers of the Tathagata, (3) all the treasury of the hidden core of the Tathagata, and (4) all the profound achievements of the Tathagata.

Nichiren interpreted the four key dharmas to be represented in the title, MYO-HO-REN-GE-KYO, or "Sutra of the Lotus Flower of the Wonderful Dharma." Besides, he understood that in the Age of Degeneration, the Bodhisattvas from Underground will certainly appear in order to propagate the Name of the Dharma. As long as Sakyamuni was physically present, the essence of the Primal Mystery *(Hommon)* was present in the "one chapter and two halves." In the evil world after his death, however, that key concept would be revealed in the five-character title of MYO-HO-REN-GE-KYO, or the "Sutra of the Lotus Flower of the Wonderful Dharma."

Nichiren also emphasized that whenever ordinary men and women accept and keep the Sacred Title, the Four Great Bodhisattvas, including Superb-Action, will unquestionably appear to protect them. Since the Sutra defines these Four

Great Bodhisattvas as "the highest leaders among people," they are destined to lead all living beings. Apparently Nichiren saw these Bodhisattvas as symbols of his own position as leader of the people. He stated this in his work, *Shoho-jisso-sho*, "The Real State of All Things."

> Born in this Age of Degeneration, [Nichiren] presents and propagates the Wonderful Dharma (the Sacred Title) prior to the appearance of Superb-Action Bodhisattva, who is initially assigned to propagate it. . . . This is a glorious thing to me. . . . It is only Nichiren who is ahead of the Bodhisattvas from Underground in performing the mission given by Sakyamuni. In this sense, [Nichiren] may also be counted as one of the Bodhisattvas from Underground (who are authorized to lead living beings in the Age of Degeneration).

Thus, the key significance of Nichiren's interpretation of the Primal Mystery *(Hommon)* lies in his belief that Superb-Action will appear in the age of the decline of the Buddha's teachings and propagate the Dharma under its title, MYO-HO-REN-GE-KYO. This view clearly reflects his own position as the leader of all living beings for the attainment of Truth today in the era of the absence of the Buddha.

Shinjo Suguro

Shinjo Suguro was born on May 1, 1925, in Tokyo, Japan, and was ordained at the age of 17. He graduated from Tokyo University, where he was in the Department of Literature. He is a former resident minister of Renshoji Temple in Katsushika, Tokyo. He was a Professor of Rissho University, in the department of Buddhist Study, and holds the degree of Ph.D. His major works are *Fundamental Problems on Nichiren Doctrine* (Kyoiku Shincho Sha), *Mahayana Buddhism* (Kosei Shuppan Sha), *Study on Early Thoughts of Concept Only* (published by Shunju Sha), all written in Japanese.

Daniel B. Montgomery

Daniel B. Montgomery has been a student of Buddhism for over forty years, specializing in Japanese Buddhism in general and Nichiren Buddhism in particular. He is the author of books and articles on the subject, including *Fire in the Lotus: The Dynamic Buddhism of Nichiren* (London, 1991) and *The Eye of the Sutra* (Tokyo, 1974). He collaborated with Bishop Senchu Murano in translating *The Lotus Sutra* into English (revised edition, Tokyo, 1991). He has also published studies in Eastern Christian mysticism.

Father Montgomery is an Archpriest of the Orthodox Church in America. For fifteen years, he was Chairman of the Foreign Language Department at the Valley Forge Military Academy. He is now retired and lives in Texas.

Nichiren Buddhist International Center

The Nichiren Buddhist International Center (NBIC) is a central facility for the propagation and missionary activities of the Nichiren Shu Order in countries outside Japan. NBIC publishes a newsletter, translates books, creates teaching materials such as pamphlets and videos, and uses Internet to spread the teachings of Nichiren Buddhism to current and prospective members worldwide.

NBIC also acts as a facility to train and educate people for the future, such as ministers from Japan, and lay members who want to become Nichiren Shu ministers. To other lay members, NBIC offers various kinds of seminars to improve their understanding and faith in Nichiren Buddhism.